Reaching the poorest

ATD Fourth World

3 UN Plaza
New York, NY 10017
USA

ISBN: 92-806-3426-7
Editions Quart Monde
15 rue Maître Albert
75005 Paris
France

Cover photograph: UNICEF/93-0686/Horner

CONTENTS

FOREWORD

UNICEF is the leading agency for children within the United Nations system. Over the past 50 years, UNICEF's work with the most disadvantaged in the countries in greatest need has marked its identity as an organization committed to the cause of children in times of peace and in times of war, working to promote consensus, encourage action, advocate in favour of the most disadvantaged and shed light on the forgotten. Long active in emergency and development activities, UNICEF has, in the last decade, also become an essential actor in the field of children's rights, embracing in particular the Convention on the Rights of the Child.

The Convention underlines that the human rights of every child are important. Each and every child has equal and inalienable rights, wherever he or she may live. For this reason, UNICEF recognizes that while it continues to be important to improve the overall situation of children in each country, it is essential to consider the specific reality of those children who have not been affected by the wave of general progress, who have remained invisible or forgotten; to promote support to those in greater need; to narrow prevailing social, economic or geographic disparities; to address girls as well as boys; to reach children living in particularly poor or remote areas as well as children who are asylum seekers or refugees, or who belong to minority or indigenous groups—indeed, all children who are vulnerable and marginalized. Similarly, while international goals or national targets remain important tools to mobilize action and resources for children, to promote improvement of their situation and achieve tangible results in a particular time-frame, they need to be considered within the broader context of the long-term process of the universal realization of the human rights of children.

In brief, with the ethical vision the Convention has brought, there is a need to address realities hitherto insufficiently considered, while sustaining achievements made in the traditional areas of development work. For this to be possible, the systematic collection, analysis and dissemination of relevant data on all these areas becomes vital. Moreover, relevant indicators need to be identified to enable trends to be assessed over time, to recognize and narrow disparities, understand and deal with the root causes of prevailing difficulties, to measure progress and to reflect human rights values, including those of equity, non-discrimination, social justice, participation and empowerment.

This book is a partial response. It describes some of the experiences of ATD Fourth World and the Permanent Forum on Extreme Poverty in the World in reaching marginalized communities by building solidarity among the people of the community as well as with outside workers who accept their role as complete partners in sharing and overcoming the enormous difficulties faced by the most disadvantaged in situations of chronic poverty.

This book presents seven case studies and the lessons to be learned from them. Three of the case studies appear in detail (Burkina Faso, Guatemala, Haiti), while the remaining four have been summarized (Canada, Peru, Thailand, Uganda). They illustrate the steps taken, the difficulties encountered, the entry points found, some success factors and the results obtained in close partnership with the poor and the communities in which they live.

The identification of challenges and the suggested solutions in this study emerged from a series of consultations between ATD Fourth World and the UNICEF Evaluation Office. The case studies were prepared by the communities and the local organizers of the seven projects, including ATD volunteers. They are often summaries of years of experience, recorded in daily notes, monthly reports and quarterly evaluations. Also, with the help of research staff at ATD Fourth World's headquarters in Pierrelaye (France), the field work has been presented in a conceptual framework that permits the comparison of similar, as well as unique, experiences.

The survey concludes that it is important, from the very beginning of development activities, to involve all members of the community, including those living in extreme poverty, in order to build a consensus in favour of an integrated programme that takes into account the rights of all community members.

We hope this book will encourage a wide exchange of experiences and lead to the development of effective new strategies for alleviating poverty.

Marta Santos Pais
Director
Division of Evaluation,
Policy and Planning
UNICEF

INTRODUCTION

In 1956, Father Joseph Wresinski (1917-1988) went to live with families sheltered in a camp for the homeless in Noisy-le-Grand (France), where living conditions were particularly trying. Impressed by the families' independence and their refusal of outside help, he founded a movement with them in 1957, which is now present on every continent.[1]

In founding this organization, Father Wresinski made a break with the traditional ways of dealing with chronic poverty. He opened up new paths and trained men and women who were able to follow them. Born into an impoverished family, Father Wresinski dedicated his life to working with the poorest. His aim was to enable them to meet the larger society on equal ground. Hence, it was no longer a case of the non-poor searching for solutions to extreme poverty, but the reverse, whereby the poor, who had been excluded from society, would work to find their place within it and make their contribution. Herein lie the originality and defining characteristic of the International Movement ATD Fourth World. Continuing the work of its founder, the Movement has worked in experimental ways to develop a partnership with the poorest. This partnership has led to a new understanding of extreme poverty, as well as the elaboration of innovative policies to eradicate it.

---

1. In 1985, Father Joseph Wresinski acknowledged the importance of the population of the Noisy-le-Grand camp: "It was those families who inspired everything I undertook for their liberation." (He was commenting on *'La rue des fleurs'*, a film made in the camp in 1960).

Father Wresinski was fully aware that the poorest are unable to effect change on their own. They must indeed be joined by others in their struggle. His permanent corps of volunteers—men and women with different backgrounds, beliefs and education—choose to link their lives to those of the poorest families. They learn to know the poor and to identify the factors that exclude them from society. The volunteers live and work in teams, going wherever the Movement needs them.

This approach to eradicating extreme poverty is focused on human investment. Father Wresinski uncovered an extraordinary wealth of human resources among those who have been shaped by poverty as well as among those who choose to work with them. Through the very resistance they continue to offer to the hardships and exclusion that afflict them, those shaped by poverty provide a wealth of resources in the struggle against extreme poverty and an invaluable contribution towards the promotion of a society respectful of the rights of all its members. Those who live and work with them, often ordinary citizens with few resources, explore new initiatives devised to create respect for the rights of the poorest. As a testimony to this spirit, the 'Permanent Forum on Extreme Poverty in the World' set up by Father Wresinski brings together citizens and small associations in more than 100 countries.

ATD Fourth World has a twofold approach: It works with the poorest, acquiring an in-depth knowledge of extreme poverty in order to carry out projects in partnership with them; while also bringing together local, national and international communities to focus on a common goal. For this purpose, it has developed evaluation and research tools, both in the field and at its international centre. The role of the centre is to bring order to the teams' various commitments and to provide the means for an objective assessment of their actions. It also seeks to make the experiences and thoughts of the poorest known to the world, accomplishing these goals through its resources, namely the House of Memory, the Action Institute and the Institute for Research and Training in Human Relations.

- *House of Memory*: Volunteers in the field write daily 'participatory observation' reports. These reports are then archived in the House of Memory, where the stories of the poorest families from all over the world are mapped, leading to a better understanding of their lives. Monographs that focus on families and communities, covering a long time period, are produced and published on the basis of such reports.[2]
- *Action Institute*: Volunteers in each team write up monthly activity reports on medium- and short-term programme planning. These are then used to evaluate the project and note the lessons learned so that future activities can be refined. The reports are kept at the Action Institute where the teams go over them with the view of developing a common approach. Every two years, evaluation/programming sessions review programmes, adjusting them when necessary and defining new objectives.
- *Institute for Research and Training in Human Relations*: The Institute conveys the history of ATD Fourth World and is set up to carry out research in various fields (health, training, citizenship, etc.) in an attempt to analyse the processes of exclusion. As a centre for training and dialogue, it aims to introduce the history, experience and thoughts of the poorest into the mainstream of contemporary thought and to place them in the context of national and international events. The Institute also edits *Revue Quart Monde*, a quarterly review, and organizes seminars, colloquiums and classes open to the general public.

---

2. As an example, we cite the study, *Familles du Quart Monde, acteurs de développement*, published in 1993 with the support of the Secretariat of the United Nations for the International Year of the Family. The study's four family histories, spanning several generations, were written together with these families. (The English translation was published in 1995 under the title, *This Is How We Live: Listening to the Poorest Families*.)

'The poorest': Defining extreme poverty

The term 'the poorest' can serve to characterize one extreme on the poverty-wealth axis; however, viewed in this way, its composition would not be clear, nor would the boundary with the adjacent category of 'less poor' be defined.

When seen in the context of a specific example, the expression 'the poorest' carries a meaning that is less theoretical and easier to define. For example, UNICEF has used the term to refer to groups that have not yet been reached by its programmes, which attempt to cover the entire population of poor people. This way of looking at the concept has at least two immediate advantages. The first is that it draws attention to the fact that part of the population is difficult if not impossible to reach. Then we must try to understand why. The second advantage is that it gives substance to the term 'the poorest' within a given community; in other words, it defines the target group.

As used by ATD Fourth World, the term 'the poorest' takes the form of a question: Who are the poorest? It is an approach rather than a designation, an approach that leads to meeting the very poor, and with them (and in a certain sense, thanks to them) meeting those who are even poorer still. This makes community development that avoids all exclusion a possibility and also helps in setting up a partnership with the poorest.

Indeed, these projects show, in very different contexts, that part of a population may be invisible because its extreme poverty keeps it excluded from the wider community. In this sense, ATD Fourth World's outreach approach echoes that of UNICEF when it notes that some members of a community fall outside the reach of its programmes.

It is an in-depth knowledge of a community—and in particular of the living conditions of its poorer members—that brings about a better understanding of the processes that lead to extreme poverty. It can also lead to discovering ways to meet the poorest members of the community effectively and to plan initiatives with them.

This approach has always been at the core of ATD Fourth World. It inspired its founder's definition of chronic poverty, which has been taken up by national and intergovernmental authorities.

> "A lack of basic security is the absence of one or more factors that enable individuals and families to assume professional, family and social responsibilities and to enjoy fundamental rights. Such a situation may become more extended and lead to more serious and permanent consequences. Chronic poverty results when the lack of basic security simultaneously affects several aspects of people's lives, when it is prolonged and when it severely compromises people's chances of regaining their rights and of reassuming their responsibilities in the foreseeable future."[3]

According to this definition, chronic poverty can be understood only in the context of the various situations of insecurity that exist within a society; for all are in fact caused by similar processes of pauperization, even if the effects can at times be more cumulative and longer lasting. This is why our approach is not intended for the elaboration of specific programmes targeting the poorest members of society; rather, it involves the community as a whole, so as to ensure that all its members can come together to foster development and solidarity.

Background to research: 'Reaching the poorest'

This research project is the result of a long collaboration between UNICEF and ATD Fourth World, both in the field and at UNICEF headquarters in New York.

---

3. See report, *Grande pauvreté et précarité économique et sociale,* French Economic and Social Council, *Journal officiel,* February 1987. (An English translation was published in 1994 as *The Wresinski Report: Chronic Poverty and Lack of Basic Security,* a report of the Economic and Social Council of France.)

See also the report presented by Leandro Despouy to the Subcommission on the Prevention of Discrimination Measures and Protection of Minorities—UN, Geneva (E/CN.4/Sub.2/1996/13).

As part of this collaboration, Father Wresinski asked the UNICEF Executive Board in 1987 to research ways of involving the poorest in development programmes, stressing that their knowledge and experience, and that of those committed to their cause over the long term, had to be taken into account.

UNICEF was one of the first United Nations agencies to express—and this took courage—the difficulty of reaching those whom development had left behind. *The State of the World's Children 1989* notes, "The challenge of reaching the very poorest is the greatest challenge in social development." When efforts are in fact made to reach them, these efforts are on a very small scale and "have often failed to reach substantial numbers among the very poorest groups."[4]

A first decision, 1989/8, entitled 'Reaching the poorest', was adopted, calling for an analysis of projects that had significantly affected the lives of the poorest in a sustainable way and for an overview of the lessons learned from these projects. Based on this decision, the Committee of Non-governmental Organizations at UNICEF focused its 1990 Forum on the issue and asked ATD Fourth World and the Permanent Forum on Extreme Poverty in the World to produce a working document on the subject. This document, 'How to Reach the Forgotten Ones?',[5] summarized the questions asked of the international community as follows:

- How do UN bodies identify the poorest populations, either already excluded from the community, or in danger of exclusion?
- Once the very poor have been identified, how do the organizations involved establish a partnership with them that will lead to an in-depth understanding of their lives?

---

4. *The State of the World's Children 1989,* UNICEF, Oxford University Press, 1989, page 57.

5. 'Comment atteindre les laissés-pour-compte?' Document written with the contribution of members of the Permanent Forum on Extreme Poverty in the World, 1990.

- How can development authorities take into account the daily realities of excluded groups?

In 1991, a second decision, 1991/6, also entitled 'Reaching the poorest', was adopted by the UNICEF Executive Board, reinforcing these same questions. In 1992, working sessions brought together staff members from the UNICEF Evaluation Office, government officials and ATD Fourth World representatives, who agreed to carry out a survey of the projects that had been launched in various countries, in order to extract lessons for future action. Having reread the project reports, they decided to focus on the conditions required to ensure the participation of the poorest groups and to foster community development based on solidarity among its members. This survey was assigned to ATD Fourth World to complete in two years.

By the end of 1992, the framework, objectives and criteria for selecting projects for review were established by the UNICEF Evaluation Office and ATD Fourth World. Thirteen projects, implemented by Fourth World teams or by members of the Permanent Forum on Extreme Poverty in the World, were submitted. Seven were selected. In 1993 and 1994, progress on the survey was regularly evaluated.

The seven projects below were the ones selected for the survey:

1. **Ouagadougou (Burkina Faso):** Participation in a country's development efforts via the 'Courtyard of a Hundred Trades', involving children and young people living on the streets.
2. **San Jacinto (Guatemala):** A community-wide effort that mobilizes a rural community for the health and well-being of all its members.
3. **Fonds-des-Nègres (Haiti):** A community development project based on a commitment with poor rural families to educate their children.
4. **Bangkok (Thailand):** A cultural project that reaches out to families afflicted by poverty and works with them in their own daily environment.

5. **Cuzco (Peru):** A university effort to carry out a research/action project with an impoverished rural population.
6. **Jinja (Uganda):** A rural project set up to register the needs of the poor and provide services to those in greatest need.
7. **Montreal and Rouyn-Noranda (Canada):** A civic project in which citizens work together in the fight against poverty.

GUIDELINES FOR ACTION

This chapter presents several courses of action shown by this study to be effective in reaching the poorest and in being reached by them. Indeed, while any particular project must focus on the local realities of a given place and on acquiring a proper knowledge of its particularities, what emerges from the overall study, given the diversity of contexts examined, is that there appear to be five basic steps that remain constant for all of the projects. We would summarize the five steps as follows:

1. Meeting a population
2. Reaching the poorest
3. Building a partnership
4. Evaluation
5. Project continuity.

1. Meeting a population

In each of these projects, the members of the team tried to know the entire community as completely as possible, while never losing sight of the importance of meeting its poorest members. An encounter of such breadth and depth requires time and means. Initially, the team got acquainted with the community, its history and culture. They also met its most disadvantaged members to learn about their lives and the hopes they harboured.

The determination to seek out the poorest was rooted in two observations that have been confirmed over and over again:

- in every group there are some members who are even poorer than the rest of the group and who, because of this extreme poverty, are more definitely excluded;

- at the same time, every community is already, in one way or another, showing solidarity with its poorest members and has some idea of how to increase the well-being of its population.

It was essential to locate people or groups who expressed such solidarity, in order to support them, for the dialogue thereby established led to concrete commitments to promote the rights of the very poor as recognized within the community, hence avoiding the pitfall of purely theoretical models.

In the first phase of the Burkina Faso project, the team discovered an informal network of people and small organizations working with children living on the streets. In Uganda, the initiative of a parish priest relied mainly on those who had always taken an active part in the fight against poverty. He sought to offer them the tools they needed. In Thailand, the team had not only begun working side by side with another organization, but had also taken the time to know and understand the ways in which the population was already supporting the very poor, in accordance with its traditions, the Buddhist tradition in particular. In Guatemala, Haiti and Peru, a similar initiative consisted in seeking out institutions (such as the school in Fonds-des-Nègres) and individuals who were committed, often behind the scenes, to the day-to-day struggle alongside the very poor. The project in Canada was interesting in this respect because its entire focus was geared towards increasing opportunities for collaboration between the very poor and those committed to working with them.

When we speak of identifying those who are active in leading the fight against extreme poverty, we should emphasize the fact that the very poor, through their daily lives, are the first ones to act in resisting poverty. Indeed, in many instances, they evidence a deep solidarity with those who are experiencing the most critical situations.

It is essential that efforts to significantly improve the lives of the very poor be rooted in efforts that the community is already making on their behalf.

2. Reaching the poorest

a) Knowledge that is rooted in the reality of the lives of the very poor

A precise definition of the word 'knowledge' is called for at this point. We are not referring here to a scientific investigation conducted with a view to acquiring knowledge of a given object. Instead, we are concerned with individuals meeting others and getting to know them in order to develop ties in a climate of mutual trust. Thus, if as part of the process of reaching the poorest, we stress the importance of a preliminary phase of acquaintance, it is because such a meeting between the team and the given population has proved to be essential not only to the inception of an initiative but also to its overall unfolding.

The development of a long-term closeness with the population constitutes a determining factor for success; it is achieved by living within the community, through participation in local community activities, by visiting people's homes, via individual or group meetings. This sharing in the daily lives of the members of the community represents a commitment through a continuing presence that makes a new future possible by reinforcing the efforts already undertaken by the poorest to release themselves from poverty.

This presence can start off by participation in programmes led by other institutions carrying out significant activities in the region, as was the case for several of our projects. In Thailand, the team collaborated with an association working with the shantytown population. In Haiti, the team supported a teaching project in a very disadvantaged rural area.

As we have already stressed above, the common objective in all these projects was to meet the poorest of the poor. It was therefore imperative not to become locked into any activity at the very outset that could potentially take up all the team's time. A common denominator for all the projects was the time devoted to meeting and developing a basis for exchange with the community.

In this respect, the example of Burkina Faso was significant. At first, the team concentrated on getting to know the young people living on the streets and their environment. They were then able to identify the children's strengths, learn about their hopes and discover their individual ways of showing mutual support; this meeting period also enabled the team to get to know other people who were already involved on behalf of the children.

Throughout the process, there was a concern for reciprocity, with as much emphasis on getting to know the population as on affording its members an acquaintance with the team that was attempting to meet with them. The projects in Canada and in Peru will both illustrate this concept, in spite of their very different contexts.

Let us note that all the projects were based on a commitment of at least 10 years. Such lasting involvement was necessary to establish relations of trust. However, burgeoning relationships were under constant threat from poverty. This held true within the community itself, and was repeatedly experienced by the very poor. And it was also true of the relationships between the poor and members of any outside agency or organization. It was therefore imperative to give the very poor an opportunity to realize that those coming to meet them truly wanted to develop a solidarity with them.

A time commitment does not in and of itself constitute a sufficient guarantee of establishing a relationship. One can live in a place for many years, have good relations with a population, provide the community with many services, and yet effect no changes that will better arm the people in the fight against poverty and exclusion. A new ambition had to be defined: that of uniting the community's existing strengths around the most deprived and their struggle against poverty.

To view the members of a group as equally poor is of no use in identifying the most disadvantaged, as the Peru project showed. The following questions had to be explicitly formulated: Who are the poorest among a given population? What is the specific reality of their lives? What are their aspirations? What efforts do they make to resist their situation? How do others support them?

Without this permanent questioning, it was impossible either to meet the poor, to get to know them in any depth or to involve them in projects that sought to foster change.

The idea of knowledge as it was elaborated in these projects highlights the importance of human investment, both on the part of the very poor and of those who have made a long-term commitment to their struggle. The daily and monthly written reports of this knowledge led to a greater appreciation of the joint challenges that lay ahead. These regular write-ups were an important tool in implementing our projects and reaching our goals. We mentioned this in the Introduction.

b) The role of a cultural project

The cases studied showed that the very poor were forced to put all their energies into the struggle for survival. They worked very hard and were often badly paid. They had to leave their communities to look for resources elsewhere. All family members needed to work to contribute to family needs. This context did not facilitate their participation in development projects. Furthermore, one consequence of the situation was that they were unable to preserve either their culture or their roots, and this was an important factor in their isolation and socio-economic exclusion.

Thus, they were often seen as incompetent, ignorant and unable to develop. They, too, came to see their situation as hopeless. Hence, any proposal for development seemed destined for others; they were unable to imagine any role in it for themselves. From the beginning, teams had to take into account this crucial reality, an intrinsic part of the heritage of the very poor, in that it confirmed the need for developing new relationships, while trying to find activities in common where the poorest could both express themselves, and demonstrate the value of their experiences and their own hopes.

"To know," wrote Father Wresinski, "is first to be conscious of being a person. It is to give a meaning to what one lives and be able to express it. It is...to know one's roots, to identify with a family, with a community. To know is to be capable of understanding one's experiences and of sharing them with others."[6] When we speak of a cultural project it is about enabling the very poor to access 'knowledge' as it is defined here. To 'know', therefore, is a prerequisite for participation in community life. In a word, this prerequisite is a condition for existence, for it can transform the poorest into full-fledged citizens enjoying to the utmost their status as individuals and as human beings.

From this point of view, all these projects provide an abundance of lessons. In four projects, the street (or field) libraries represented a response to the necessity for the very poor to have access to this kind of knowledge. The facilitators approached the children with books and activities, such as painting and drawing, guiding them towards discovery by encouraging the children to participate and giving them the means to express their feelings and to question others. In so doing, they introduced a new set of relationships into the heart of family and social life, opening them up to the outside world, while revealing their creative abilities. Given that the parents were involved in the process, their children's future was quite naturally addressed. Strengthened by a dialogue in which others took their hopes into account and to which they could actively contribute, the very poor parents gained the confidence required to involve themselves in development projects.

The leaders of the projects in Peru and Uganda found different paths towards similarly privileged relationships with the poorest of a community by taking the time to develop original activities with them. They sought ways for the very poor to regain their self-confidence and acquire the means to communicate their hopes to other community members. In that spirit, Rouyn-Noranda Crossroads in Quebec was specifically geared towards encouraging individuals who had lived in chronic poverty to join others

---

6. *Revue Igloos-Quart Monde,* 'The child of the Fourth World on a quest for knowledge', No. 105-106, 2nd quarter, 1979.

with the same experience, in order to draw new strengths from their common experience of exclusion and develop the confidence to participate in collective projects.

c) Joining the poorest in their aspirations

In a community mired in widespread poverty, where basic needs for water, health care and schools are not met, everyone's concerns must receive attention. The extent to which progress for the community at large might reach the poorest of its members remains an issue. Indeed, many programmes were conceived for a population as a whole, and not with the view of reaching every last member of the group. It is therefore not unusual for programmes to set 70 per cent of the population as their target, the remainder often including the most disadvantaged, those who, for one reason or another, were not able to take part in the programme as it was set up.

It is important to note here that simply identifying and meeting the poorest in no way guarantees their participation in a project. A certain number of conditions must be met to make that possible. The duration of a commitment is one condition, and we have also emphasized the importance of a cultural project. However, to genuinely and effectively reach the poorest, one must go beyond an assessment of community-wide concerns. The daily reality of the poorest and the hopes they carry deep in their hearts have to be considered. It should be noted that the harsh living conditions in which the poorest labour have two consequences. The first is that the living conditions characteristic of extreme poverty foster specific aspirations. The poorest members have the same fundamental needs as the rest of the community (water, health care, education, etc.), and yet they may experience them differently. They may also be lacking things that have already been provided for other members of the community. In order to satisfy their own needs, the poorest might also require other resources, adapted to their own realities. The second consequence is that the poorest scarcely have the means even to express their aspirations.

For these reasons, both the process of joining in, and its explanation, are fundamental.

The issues described above shaped the infant malnutrition programme in Guatemala. In Fonds-des-Nègres (Haiti), they determined the school's original function as well as its programme and evolution. Likewise, in Ouagadougou, the team balanced the ambitions of the Burkina Faso nation as a whole, while remaining close to the lives of the poorest children and youths to whom they had made a commitment. Despite the very different context in Bangkok, the process was similar.

d) Promotion of the family as an objective

Yet another aspect of the lives of the poorest has to be taken into account when implementing any programme that is intended to reach them. We have observed a deep sense of family ties among the poorest, even though these ties are constantly being eroded by the extreme poverty of their lives. The Burkina Faso project was certainly the most striking example of this.

Initially, the project focused on children and young people living on the streets, some of whom had not seen their families for many years. As they got to know them better, the team gradually realized that all of these young people wanted to renew contact with their families. So overriding was this desire that the most important thing was to help them make contact as soon as possible.

It is essential to understand the role of the family (whatever its model) in the struggle against poverty. Indeed, poverty generates such deprivation that it often ends up preventing a human being from living with others in dignity. Over time, such poverty destroys family and social life. Experience has shown that a project aimed at reaching the poorest should propose, from the very beginning, to establish conditions that will lead to a better family life, since individuals feel the greatest level of responsibility for those closest to them.

Questions regarding family security (resources, work, housing, health, education), and the potential of the families to participate in projects are crucial and therefore at the top of the initial agenda. These concerns had to be translated into concrete objectives (such as the Nutrition Centre in San Jacinto, Guatemala) in the projects we are examining. They then became part of a contract between the most disadvantaged families, the rest of the community and other partners involved in these programmes.

e) Building consensus

We have emphasized the fact that it is necessary to know and to take into account the hopes of the very poor, while at the same time remaining aware of the hopes of the other members of a community where widespread poverty exists. The question that then arises is how to build a consensus between the different groups.

Experience has taught us that if the will to reach the poorest is not there from the very outset, if it is not an integral part of the common goals of a community, it is very difficult to enlist the members of the community in an initiative, even though they stand to be beneficiaries as much as partners. Carrying out a project of this sort requires a thorough education, for it challenges customary ways of proceeding. In fact, for such a project to succeed within a given community, all those involved must simultaneously evaluate the potential meaning of the action for the poorest and their own role within the project. This implies learning to communicate with them, treating them as partners, as well as including them in the elaboration, implementation and evaluation processes.

The example of Burkina Faso shows how the team members, after spending the time required to familiarize themselves with the context, were able to propose a project in which children living on the streets fulfilled a central role from the outset and were able to make themselves useful to others. The projects in Guatemala and Uganda highlight the fact that consensus can be built only by integrating the concerns of an entire community afflicted by poverty.

3. Building a partnership

We have seen how to set up a project by making use of an already existing dynamic consisting, on the one hand, of the efforts and acts of solidarity demonstrated by the very poor themselves, and on the other, of the commitment of those working side by side with them. Ambitious programmes and new policies within given communities (local as well as national and international) must be created on this basis. The stakes in the projects described above consisted in fostering consensus among the partners, including the poorest members, around a number of objectives devised to control poverty and put an end to its most extreme forms.

This mobilization was a component of the programmes of all the projects featured in this study from the very outset. Initiated with the local authorities, it was further extended, according to the opportunities afforded each situation, to larger institutions and international organizations. For example, the 'Centre for Creativity and Encounters' opened in the neighbourhood of Tha Ding Daeng in Bangkok thanks to a collaboration between the International Labour Organization (ILO), the Ministry of Labour and ATD Fourth World. Let us note that to achieve such results take time (several years in this particular case) because each partner needs to set its own pace (with the population involved included among the partners). But there is also a concern to establish rapidly a dialogue with others likely to get involved in a sustainable anti-poverty programme. Other examples can be cited, such as UNICEF's contribution to the Ouagadougou project. All the projects, in fact, included multiple partnerships.

Particular attention needed to be paid to establishing a partnership with the poorest. Partnership entails more than just a good temporary cooperation centred around a specific activity. A partnership of this nature should also show clearly that the poor have an important role to play in the larger community. In that sense, they are not only a target to be reached but also human beings to be empowered in such a way as to help them find a worthy place within the group, for the greater benefit of the entire community.

Two examples illustrate this point. In Burkina Faso, young people living on the streets practised a number of techniques at the Courtyard of a Hundred Trades. In one workshop, they produced teaching materials for pre-schools with few resources. In Haiti, parents in isolated villages took it upon themselves to contribute to their children's education by building small traditional huts to serve as rural schools. In these two situations, people who were looked down upon because they were very poor helped their families' and communities' dreams come true and also contributed to the achievement of the goals set by their national governments.

When men and women who have known extreme poverty are given the opportunity to learn how to show publicly that every human being is worthy of respect (as in the Canadian project) or to form committees (as in Guatemala, Haiti and Peru), they become part of a social transformation. They give proof of their ability to become, with others, agents of development for their communities.

The stakes of such partnerships need to be explicitly stated. The participants in the Quebec project were convinced that winning the fight against extreme poverty required a shift from assistance to partnership. But partnership with the poorest cannot consist of enlisting their participation in a project conceived without them. They must take part in the planning of a project for the benefit of the whole of society, a project that relies on the skills they have acquired precisely because of the extreme conditions in which they lived and which contributed to their marginalization.

This marginalization is apparent in the lack of access to the goods and services that are available to the rest of the community. Every community has infrastructures and services, more or less developed, that are designed to meet the community's vital needs. Those whose extreme poverty deprives them of access to these services are at a serious disadvantage, as was shown in all the projects that were part of the exploratory study. Improving the access of the poor to these services was an absolute priority, not only to better their living conditions, but also to open up the possibility of their participation in individual, family and societal projects. This was achieved in all the projects and required an ongoing collaboration with the individuals whose institutions supplied services. This was possible only after having gained a greater understanding of the very poor and created closer ties with the institutions concerned.

A brief explanation of what was done in San Jacinto (Guatemala) in order to improve the access of the poorest to health care illustrates the process. The team got to know the very poor of the community, using the method described. When the team became convinced that a health care project was necessary, they began working with the local health services, a collaboration that led to common experiences on which to base an understanding of the lives of the very poor. Indeed, a key factor in the success of all projects is this twofold approach in which a real common effort is actively pursued by both the population and the providers. This was necessary in order to discover what prevented the poor from benefiting from services in the first place; conversely, an awareness of the constraints on service providers was also important. A proper assessment of these variables in turn helped determine what strategies should be adopted in order to facilitate access of the very poor to the services in question. In this process, the team could not limit itself to a dialogue with the representatives of the providers; the very poor had to become an integral part of this partnership as well. In other words, the final objective was to enable the very poor to become direct partners with the providers themselves.

Other projects in different fields provide similar examples. In Ouagadougou, the 'health hut' project in the Courtyard of a Hundred Trades was a close collaboration with the local health centre. In Canada, the Rouyn-Noranda Crossroads again sought to enable the poorest to become partners with the services they used. In Cuzco (Peru), the project worked to give poor peasants 'ownership' of certain local services, thereby enabling the local people truly to benefit from those services.

To conclude this discussion, we should emphasize the need to train those who intervene on behalf of the most disadvantaged groups, so that they can effectively identify those who are the most excluded and work with them. Only when this training is taken seriously is progress possible. The Quebec project offers an example of what can be accomplished in this area and illustrates the direct rôle of the given population in providing training of this type.

4. Evaluation

For evaluation purposes, variables measuring the efficacy of change should be factored in at the beginning of the project. In particular, variables must be identified to gauge the role of the poorest in the project and the amount of progress they made.

Planning: Towards achieving significant goals

Classic criteria were used in noting the progress of a project, for example the percentage of children in school, or immunization coverage, or the number of children attending the Courtyard of a Hundred Trades. Such criteria helped to ascertain if progress had been made in achieving fixed objectives. It was necessary, however, to add new elements—at times more difficult to establish—so as to measure the participation of the poorest. Several of the projects can be used as examples of this.

a) In Haiti

For the school in Fonds-des-Nègres, the primary criteria were:

- the number of children attending school;
- the number of children completing the primary grades;
- the number of teachers who received training, either in their speciality or in how to build a partnership with parents;
- the number of children enrolled in school from families where no child had ever attended school before. These children's progress in school was followed with particular attention. This attention is in and of itself a way of fine-tuning the initial criteria;

- the number of parents involved in the parents' committees.

Although the same criteria were used for the most disadvantaged families, the specificity of their situation required additional criteria. We looked, for instance, at the extent to which school participation took them out of the isolation brought on by extreme poverty and led them to take active roles in community life. Another example, which had not been one of the pre-established criteria, was to be found in those teachers who had received training and yet who had given up the idea of leaving their village. Even though leaving would have meant personal advancement, they chose to remain a part of the project in the village, providing an interesting way of measuring the mobilization of others around the poorest.

b) In Guatemala

Criteria for the nutritional centre were:

- the number of families participating and the rate of attendance;
- the level of malnutrition in the village where the centre was located;
- immunization coverage, which reflected families' participation in preventive programmes offered by local services;
- mothers' participation rates;
- the psychomotor development measured by the centre's preschool activities.

The rate of attendance of very poor families at local health centres (in particular the health post in San Jacinto) showed to what extent, in a project based on multiple partnership, families were able to take back 'ownership' of the services. Each partner could then place itself in relation to the progress made. Making use of these common evaluations, health post staff adjusted their activities (at least temporarily) in order to ensure that the health technician would be more frequently available to communities situated away from the village centre.

c) In Burkina Faso

Besides criteria aimed at evaluating the number of children at the Courtyard of a Hundred Trades, it was also important to assess how many had acquired a skill. The evaluation also looked at how the project enabled participating children to show their solidarity with other children also living on the streets. Criteria had been introduced relating to health. Little by little, the team's attention was focused on how children re-established ties with their families. This had emerged as one of the children's major concerns, even in those cases where contact had been completely cut off, the break having occurred long ago. Although this goal may seem remote with respect to the original aims of the project, it illustrates the determination to reshape a project according to the true needs of the poorest.

We note that all the projects made a conscious effort to fine-tune their evaluations, advancing from classic criteria of participation and progress (numbers enrolled in school, percentage of children finishing primary school) to criteria evaluating the position of very poor families within the community and the community's behaviour towards its most disadvantaged members. Such variables were naturally more difficult to isolate and required a keen awareness of signs demonstrating a change of outlook and new initiatives.

This evaluation process, which went beyond the usual practices, was based on a series of simple questions, namely: In what ways had the poorest progressed towards greater independence and freedom? Had they acquired the means to fulfil their responsibilities within their communities? What conditions had been created to ensure that the poorest themselves could contribute to the solutions? Regular evaluations led to the updating of goals as well as a reassessment of criteria for the evaluations themselves.

Working methods

For each point that was examined we tried to find the working methods that seemed to facilitate progress and also those that seemed on the contrary to hinder development. An analysis of the different categories of effects observed from these various methods was likewise undertaken.

For example, evaluations of all seven projects highlighted the positive effects of certain working methods. Their presence in one project after another makes them significant enough to warrant the summary that follows:

- the commitment of the people running a project, which led them to invest the time and means needed to meet very poor families and to ensure their participation. Over the years, this practice created a spirit of shared responsibility in the community and contributed to mobilizing everyone around the community's common goals;
- the fact that enough time was given at the outset in order to really get to know the community and its poorest members. The projects then corresponded more realistically to the needs of the community, even when the situation seemed urgent and immediate action was called for. In Guatemala, for example, faced with a community suffering from malnutrition, this type of approach was behind the idea for a pre-school, which motivated the most malnourished families to participate, and in fact made it succeed. And in Burkina Faso, talking with children who live on the streets, not so much about what they needed and what they lacked, but about their desire to regain a meaningful relationship with their families and with society in general, led to a profound change in the children's self-image and the community's view of them.

Difficulties encountered

When examining the difficulties encountered, it is important to remember that the pattern of insecurity entrenched in the lives of the poorest can prevent them from taking advantage of opportunities for change, improvement and development and even stop them from becoming involved at all.

Certain other difficulties revealed by the evaluation process should also be mentioned. In Haiti, the need to train teachers was not clearly understood at the beginning of the programme, and this delayed the creation of a stable and competent teaching corps. In Uganda, the community's lack of funds halted the establishment of services that the local community saw as priorities. In this particular instance, the obstacle was a lack of external support.

When, because of budgetary restrictions, private or public sponsors cut financial support—without having examined the projects—for a research/action project in Peru and for social benefits in Canada, the survival of the programmes was compromised. These actions demonstrated a lack of understanding of the time needed for the deployment of human and material resources adapted to the needs of the very poor.

It should also be emphasized that in the fight against extreme poverty nothing can ever be taken for granted. Advances that seem firmly established can be compromised by local factors. A project's success can be limited by an unfavourable economy, a disinvestment in social programmes, a change in personnel with new staff coming in who may be less inclined to grant priority to the poorest or even when a set of improvements in one aspect of life is not reinforced by improvements in other sectors. All this shows how little understanding there still is of the need for global policies to put an end to poverty and exclusion.

In fact, permanent vigilance must be exercised in assessing the extent to which the needs of the most disadvantaged populations are being met, or on the contrary denied, as well as in evaluating the changes effected by specific initiatives. Which is why we have stressed the importance of regular and rigorous evaluations, so as to estimate the progress made in relation to the goals targeted and to consider possible modifications to the course of action. These evaluations should be an opportunity for a given population to provide direct input into the project through active participation. In this way, they can contribute to all aspects of a project's success. Their own involvement in the evaluation guarantees that the project will take into account the reality of the poorest and remain faithful to their hopes. Ultimately, it is a way to acknowledge them as true and indispensable partners.

5. Project continuity

Any project geared towards significantly changing the lives of the very poor and their place in the community must take a long-term view. Beyond the consensus required to implement initiatives, people involved must remain in place to ensure continuity, in order to guarantee lasting changes in favour of the poorest. A follow-up of this type does not mean pursuing the same initiative. Indeed, some projects are designed solely to provide an initial impetus to change. Subsequent activities are then carried out in a different manner. In this context, the follow-up aspect, whether it initiates new activities or simply assures a continued presence, should guarantee that the partnership with the most disadvantaged retains its original spirit.

If it is to be effective, this follow-up should be planned for at the very outset of any project. It should in fact become an extension of the initial mobilization of the community for the project, and be part of it. Let us add that project continuity requires a financial investment. Finding subsidies for a short- or medium-term pilot project is always easier than securing the means to sustain its progress within a society. Attitudes concerning the question must be changed; the opportunity is definitely ripe for a dialogue with funding organizations on the issue.

The school project in Haiti was planned around a general mobilization to guarantee long-term autonomy for the project; today, the follow-up is in its final stage. In San Jacinto, Guatemala, the team is no longer directly on the spot, but a network of 'continuity' people ensures the vitality of the partnership with the poorest. In Burkina Faso, the health project, which from the beginning was in collaboration with local partners, is now entirely in the hands of local structures.

THE COURTYARD OF A HUNDRED TRADES

Burkina Faso: Case study

- A partnership with young people living on the streets
- Young people: Bridge to the most disadvantaged
- A partnership for children living on the streets
- Guidelines for action

The International Movement ATD Fourth World's presence in Burkina Faso dates back to a 1979 meeting between the founder of the 'Arche', Jean Vanier, and the founder of the International Movement ATD Fourth World, Father Joseph Wresinski. As a result of this meeting, the Movement put two of its long-term volunteers[7] *at the disposal of the Maison de l'Arche in Ouagadougou for a period of two years. During that period, the volunteers met with numerous committed people of Burkina Faso who were working with population groups living in very difficult circumstances. These people were invited to share their experiences and questions at an international seminar organized by the Movement at UNESCO headquarters in Paris on the topic of 'Extreme Poverty and Exclusion in Africa'. The project described here arose out of that seminar.*

---

7. The International Movement ATD Fourth World Volunteer Corps is made up of men and women of different countries, social backgrounds, convictions and beliefs. Their professional backgrounds are equally diverse: They may have been trained as carpenters, sociologists, secretaries or social workers, to cite just a few examples. For a period ranging from two years to a lifetime, they place their skills at the service of very disadvantaged populations, together carrying out projects and conducting research with them.

1. A partnership with young people living on the streets

In July 1982, with the agreement and support of friends in Burkina Faso, another International Movement ATD Fourth World volunteer came to Ouagadougou.[8] His goal was to make friends with children and young people who, left to their own devices and apparently without family ties, form groups on the streets of the capital city, and live under particularly difficult conditions (in terms, for instance, of housing, employment and health). From the outset, he chose not to involve himself directly in the survival of these children and young people (e.g., not to distribute food or medicine), in order to avoid becoming trapped in an assistance-oriented behaviour that would ignore existing informal support systems within the country and the life experiences of the individuals in question.

A prolonged phase of mutual acquaintance

This volunteer sought to encourage any ties that he could establish with the young people on a informal basis. He went to the post office daily to collect his mail, to the central market to do his shopping, to the offices of the water and electric companies to pay his bills and, in short, to all those places where children and especially young people spend their days trying to earn a living by watching vehicles or providing services (baggage carrying, selling items on the streets, shining shoes, etc.).

The ties developed day by day were initially kept distant, in order to establish a mutual acquaintance based on respect and dignity, i.e., respect for the young people's 'working hours', their families and their less well-regarded companions. Eliciting

8. This volunteer joined the two other volunteers whom Father Joseph Wresinski had sent to Jean Vanier's 'Arche'. An engineer by training, he had several years of experience working with disadvantaged families.

the stories of the children's[9] lives in all their wretched detail, in the name of securing so-called field knowledge, was avoided. The time had not yet come to develop a project with them. What was needed was to give them the time at the beginning to discover that the volunteer belonged to a movement of solidarity with the world's very disadvantaged families, founded by a man who had himself been born into poverty, Father Joseph Wresinski.

The volunteer sought to make all of these encounters with the children meaningful despite their brevity. He made a point of greeting each person with a handshake and learning his or her name. He asked after the ones who were absent and clearly expressed his concern for each and every one of them, including those who might easily have been forgotten. In this way, he gradually became acquainted with different aspects of their lives: Today, so-and-so was at such-and-such a place where he had found such-and-such a job; someone else was lying ill in the hideaway where he usually spent the night.

Because he was aware that his attitude in these first contacts would affect the future development of the relationships, the volunteer avoided responding immediately to individual requests for assistance. He systematically asked: "What do you usually do in this situation? Whom can you turn to for help?" This led him to discover the existence of a whole informal network of people who maintained periodic relationships with these children, such as street-sellers operating from stalls, and civil servants whose paths crossed theirs. The children were in fact proud to introduce these people. A direct gratification of their requests would have eroded this existing support network. In addition to providing assistance from time to time, these relationships afforded the children a tenuous opening into the adult

9. The terms 'children' and 'young people' will be used interchangeably. Those frequenting the Courtyard range from 8 to 25 years in age.

world and sometimes contributed to maintaining the remnants of a link to one or another member of their own families.

Within a short period of time, the children began seeking out the volunteer. In these contacts, he tried to be their friend and to see the children as whole persons, rather than simply through their various needs. All too often, people would attempt to establish relationships with them that, in effect, rendered them dependent on the assistance provided or even abused their confidence. In one such case, a reporter invited a group of children out to eat one day and then took advantage of their trust to film them that night sleeping on the street, without asking their consent. After this incident, one of the children expressed his distress in these words: "What will my parents and relatives say now? I've ruined the family name."

The experience showed that the meagreness of the volunteer's resources was an asset to him in becoming better acquainted with the children's strengths and hopes. Some of them took the initiative of helping him, rather than continuing to see what they could obtain from him. One child would come to advise him on caring for trees; other children would spontaneously begin sweeping the courtyard where he lived or adjacent areas, revealing their eagerness to establish friendship and escape dependency. They were now in a position to make themselves useful, and they were proud of it.

Seeking support within the country

Along with this phase of getting to know the children, an effort was being made to establish contact with those individuals who, within the framework of either public or private organizations, worked with these children or with the very poor in general. A great deal of time was given to developing relations with individuals who showed particular concern for these children's future and would therefore be likely to participate in a project or, at the very least, to agree to meet with the children.

As a result of these efforts, in early 1983 four young adults, known either through the Social Committee[10] of the neighbourhood parish youth group or through the young people on the streets themselves, became involved in this process of getting acquainted with the children. Gradually making friends with the children, they have since been joined by others over the years. The term 'friends' as used in this report was preferred over that of 'volunteers', which did not hold much meaning in Burkina Faso. In addition, the people involved spontaneously defined themselves as such.

Learning more about work experiences

In July 1983, seeking to develop an understanding of the children's lives and hopes on which to base a common project, this small team began a street survey of the young people regarding a concern that seemed essential and remained family related: work.

The collective interest in this survey displayed on the part of the young people was surprising. Those already interviewed would go in search of other respondents. Groups of up to 20 children would form to discuss the subject. Some young people would make energetic efforts to assemble the children present to join in the discussion. Once retranscribed and translated, excerpts from these interviews were collected in an album illustrated by the young people. For the first time, their voices were being heard.

This in-depth approach yielded several facts concerning work. First, almost all of these young people had experienced nothing but failure, particularly in the context of work relations, in which they found a total lack of respect. At the same time, they clearly expressed a desire to be recognized as workers, even though they were aware that the various tasks they had performed did not constitute real jobs with a future. Some even went so far as to say

10. A group of people in John XXIII Parish who organized various projects to help Ouagadougou's needy.

that, as a result of the accumulated humiliation, they were no longer looking for work.

From these different findings, it was determined that any work-related project with the children should have two priority goals:

1. Providing the young people with a positive work experience, however brief, the main goal being to enable them to feel capable, at least for a given period of time, of achieving something of quality with their hands and of belonging to a team of workers. An experience of this sort would enable them to regain confidence in their abilities and at the same time discover how much the working world had to offer.
2. Making certain that young people's success would not cut them off from their comrades seeking similar success, but on the contrary become a matter of pride and encouragement for the whole group.

The event that gave rise to the Courtyard of a Hundred Trades

Shortly before Christmas 1983, a group of young people from the central market asked if they could hold a party in the courtyard where the volunteer lived. They specifically asked that only members of their own group be allowed to participate in it so as to avoid any conflicts. At the time, tensions were running high between various groups in the city.

The volunteer accepted no compromise on this point. For the party to take place, the priority would be to bring in the children with the most difficult lives, whoever they might be, and everyone would have to help. The children giving the party would also have to share the expenses with the disadvantaged families in the neighbourhood, which was possible for everyone. The young people then suggested that a contribution cost be set, insisting that it should apply to everyone, and that they would come and prepare the meal themselves. The friends worked hard to give this celebration a family atmosphere and to encourage the different groups to meet and get along together through activities such as organizing the meal, performances and dancing.

This event might seem insignificant. Yet in fact, it sparked the project that would later be called the 'Courtyard of a Hundred Trades', by clearly demonstrating the children's need to be fully recognized, and to join forces for projects that would allow no exclusion. From the start, whatever the activity, the young people would be partners, not beneficiaries, and each and every one of them, from the leader to the least accepted child, would be asked to reach out to those in greater need.

How the workshops began

Launching the first construction project

The first construction project was launched in May 1984 in the courtyard where the volunteer lived. The goal was to put up two types of roughcast buildings: a 'permanent' shelter and a closed structure. These were designed specifically for the young people's activities. There was also a room set aside for office work and for welcoming visitors.

Fully aware of the importance of this first effort to the entire project that they wanted to develop with the young people, and in spite of the fear of failure, everyone—volunteers and friends alike—made a clear choice: Instead of recruiting the most enterprising and those most likely to succeed, they offered this work to the four young people who seemed the least well regarded and the most discouraged. Here again, it was important to prove that everyone, and first and foremost the most disadvantaged, belonged in the project. Furthermore, because of the great difficulties that they were experiencing, these young people were probably the most likely to inspire new hope in their peers: "If even *he* can manage to do real work, then *I* must be able to, too!"

Lastly, they would be evidence to the outside world of the courage and determination to learn on the part of not just some, but *all*, of the young people living on the streets.

Carrying out the project

Initially estimated at one and a half months, construction actually took two and a half months, but all of the work planned was completed. In addition, and this is essential, the four young people managed to stick with it to the end, and on a regular basis. They were all present at least two thirds of the time; one of them missed 10 days, and another only 2 days.

Evaluation with the young people

Achieving partnership with the young people was not a simple matter. Because they were not used to speaking out in front of their peers and adults, they had trouble expressing themselves during evaluation meetings.

For a start, the young people expressed their satisfaction at learning, and at feeling that they were making progress towards acquiring a real trade. They hoped to continue to train, whether in construction or in any other trade with prospects for a future. They also stressed their satisfaction at getting along well both among themselves and with the workman. Their words showed, moreover, that by 'getting along', they meant much more than keeping the peace. For them, this also included the feeling of being respected and treated like any other worker. It made them aware of their worth and gave them a renewed sense of self-confidence.

The young people mentioned only one real difficulty, but it was one of great importance to them: the fact that they were not understood by the young people not participating in the construction project. Their comrades put them down: Why had they agreed to do tiring work that took the whole day and paid a lot less than their usual activities? This lack of understanding was hard for the young people to bear and often became a source of discouragement. However, they themselves were quick to grasp the meaning of the work that they were accomplishing, and this undoubtedly prevented them from giving up during the most difficult moments.

Foundations laid for the next stage of the project

At the evaluation meetings, the young people explained what the work meant to them:

- recovering their pride by presenting another image of themselves to the outside world;
- regaining hope in the future by learning a real trade that would allow them to be independent and start a family. As one youth put it simply: "You have to have work to have money. And when you don't have money, you can't have a wife."
- being able to consider re-establishing ties with their families.

Apart from its positive effect on the young people, this project was decisive for the future of the programme because it provided the grounds for mutual trust.

Adjusting the workshops to the young people's input

Other workshops aimed at providing an introduction and initiation to a trade, bringing young people into contact with an artisan and allowing them to create something together, followed this first undertaking in 1984. Covering fields as diverse as carpentry, pottery, bronze work, sewing and making batiks, these workshops were part time and short term, not permanent. Open to younger children, they quickly became the central element of the whole project, the one that gave it the name of Courtyard of a Hundred Trades.

While each one of these workshops was unique, depending on the type of work and the personalities of the young people and artisans involved, a few constants gradually emerged and guided the team towards a more comprehensive plan of action.

However, no such plan would have been possible without the progress that had been achieved in the evaluations with the young people. After much experimenting, the team decided to hold only a single evaluation meeting at the end of each workshop, and to base it on specific, prepared questions. Changes were made in the workshops on the basis of these evaluations. They went from two or three weeks in the beginning to six weeks on average, because the young people felt they needed at least that much time to assimilate what they were learning.

Towards a goal of family reunification

In contrast to what one generally hears on the street, the evaluation meetings with the young people brought out the tremendous importance that they attached to their families.

Participation in a workshop turned out to be an ideal opportunity for renewing ties. Strengthened by their recovered dignity, many children would ask the team to go with them to see their families. "Otherwise, they won't believe us when we speak of our lives," they would add. Some who had had a harder time or were faced with particularly difficult family situations insisted on the importance of such combined efforts. Conscious of the fragile nature of this renewed hope, the children did not want to wait until the end of the training course, however short. The team discovered that some of the young people had not seen their parents for 5, 10 or even 15 years, to the point where some parents even believed them to be dead. These highly intense encounters revealed the children's tremendous longing for forgiveness and their desire to renew their family ties while keeping their own self-respect.

In addition, the first meetings with parents showed how deeply they too wished to see their children again and how affected they were by these reunions where everybody's feelings were respected, thus confirming that the young people had put the volunteers and friends on the right track. Even if it would take a long time for most of the youths to be able to talk about their families and find a way to achieve reconciliation, this would remain central to the project.

The need for a long-term effort

It must be acknowledged that while, in retrospect, the prolonged phase of getting to know the young people was clearly worth while, the volunteers and friends found it a challenge at the time. As the months went by, they had to resist growing pressure to 'do something' right away.

It should be noted also that, in attempting to form a partnership with the children and young people, they were asking a lot of the youths. Because of the energy that they were already investing in day-to-day survival, the young people were searching more for someone on whom to lean and a ready-made project in which to participate rather than to have to put additional energy into a joint effort. It took great perseverance on the part of the volunteers and friends to continue seeking out the young people's opinions rather than simply going with their own vision of the project.

All of this took place within the increasingly difficult economic situation of the country at that time. Several years of drought, a decline in purchasing power and a rise in unemployment combined to produce an appreciable deterioration in the young people's living conditions and to heighten their concern for their own futures.

2. Young people: Bridge to the most disadvantaged

Although the first concern in reaching out to the young people was to support them in their desire to change their lives, it became clear that the Courtyard of a Hundred Trades project had higher ambitions. Indeed, far from limiting itself to simply enlisting the young people as partners in a vocational training or family reunification programme, the project sought to help them enable others in even greater need to regain confidence in their lives and in their capabilities. In an even wider sense, they needed to be able to take their part in their country's development and to prove their own solidarity with families mired in the cycle of extreme poverty.

The challenge of including the children in greatest need in the Courtyard of a Hundred Trades

In discussing the 1983 Christmas party, we mentioned the children's concerns about different groups mixing. The challenge of bringing more disadvantaged children into the Courtyard of a Hundred Trades was manifested daily in various forms: confrontations between different groups, bullying of smaller children by bigger ones and, perhaps most serious, rejection of some children by others. Invariably, those rejected were the weakest. Dirtier, more poorly dressed, ill or less resourceful, they were ideal scapegoats. In some cases, it was their family history that provoked the taunts. The nicknames given to them were revealing: 'the crazy woman's kid', 'Little Lunatic', etc.

Friendship for the weakest did not come naturally to the young people, even if compassion sometimes won out. The words of one youth at the start of a workshop pointed up the problem: "If people like Oumarou come, it's no good. He's got flies following him. He's got a wound that stinks."

For young people who had regained their self-respect and had therefore begun to pay attention to their hygiene and health and to aspire to recognition as workers, it was not easy to have to mix with others who reminded them of their failures and put them to shame in front of the outside world. While a reaction of this sort was understandable, accepting it was out of the question. The message that the Courtyard of a Hundred Trades wanted to get across was that all children without exception had their own worth and that, for children to succeed fully, they needed the support of their families, regardless of the state of those families.

Nevertheless, imposing the presence of a child that the others tended to exclude was possible only if volunteers, friends and young people all shared a certain mindset. This meant, of course, taking into consideration every aspect of the children's lives.

The health programme as an example of solidarity with the neediest

This focus on the most disadvantaged was widely illustrated in the area of health.

The issue of the children's health had been among the team's primary concerns. As early as 1982, an extra volunteer had started to provide health care on a very informal basis to children living on the streets outside of her working hours, liaising with another association. Finally, formalizing this effort, a more structured health care component was put in place in 1986. It was based on two elements:

- providing twice-weekly health care hours, supplemented by regular question-and-answer sessions with a qualified individual on the health topics of greatest concern to the children.
- contacting the various city medical facilities that might serve the children (dispensaries, the hospital and laboratories) in order to collaborate with their efforts to give the children access to care.

Using a one-room Health Hut that the children had built in the Courtyard of a Hundred Trades, ATD Fourth World took on all aspects of health care that would normally have been provided for by families, working to make the various services more accessible to children.

In addition to helping the children surmount their feelings of powerlessness over their wretched living conditions and noticeably improving their state of health, the programme elicited many individual actions that attested to the population's concern for their well-being. This concern was largely shared by the public services, despite their serious lack of resources and the absence of the family support on which the medical system traditionally relied.

The initiative evolved around a double imperative: removing the obstacles to the children's access to health care while at the same time reaffirming the importance of the small actions that enabled the children to take charge of their health, e.g., helping a sick friend by getting food for him, heating water to wash his wound, taking up a collection to pay for his taxi to the hospital, etc. It was remarkable to see how much a child benefited from being able to extend a gesture of solidarity to one worse off than himself. This desire to be useful to others turned out to be more motivating than, for example, purely personal success in securing access to training.

As we have stated, the health programme provided an opportunity to expand the challenge of providing health care access to cover all children living in particularly insecure conditions in the city of Ouagadougou, in that it allowed us to confront the children and young people with their responsibility to defend *everyone's* right to health care. For what would be the point of various friends' mobilizing the community to facilitate their access to health care if the youths themselves did not extend this access to the children they met? And who knew better than they of other children living on their own, rejected because of their diseases, disabilities or backgrounds and hiding away to escape the pressures of the city?

The health programme thus contributed to expanding the team's awareness of a number of children suffering hardship. The programme's first effect was to dispel the children's belief that disease was inevitable. Later, it brought them an increased sense of responsibility, empowering the children to take charge of their own health. It also caused them to become more demanding about their own health care, an attitude that carried the risk of turning them into "privileged children" who would no longer care what happened to others. That is why it was important to initiate meetings, at times painful to the children, in order to examine ways in which each one could help to improve the common lot: by sweeping the courtyard upon arrival, by offering to clean the Health Hut, by washing the clothes of a child who was ill and too tired to do it himself, by giving an 'unknown' child a chance to get to know the Courtyard and helping him to meet the team—all the many unforgettable actions that increased the children's stature in their own eyes and in the eyes of their country. One child, for example, proudly told of how he had tricked a hesitant child into coming to the Courtyard of a Hundred Trades for health treatment by making him think that they were only going begging together! The children's own experiences gave them the ability to find ways of dealing with different situations.

It was therefore important to encourage all these actions and to make sure that the children did not confine them to their close friends but instead reached out to all those in the city who needed their help. In order to achieve this, all the children's efforts on behalf of others had to be reaffirmed and encouraged as much as possible, for example during the children's own meetings or in public discussions.

As a result of this health programme—designed to mobilize children on behalf of their peers and make outside contacts with the health service providers—the Ministry of Health held a 'community health worker' training seminar in 1992 for some 30 young people chosen by their peers. In 1993, the AEMO (Action d'éducation en milieu ouvert/Open Education Programme) team, under the Ministry of Social Action and Family, took over the running of the Health Hut.

Seeking participation in the country's development through specific events

Different opportunities for children and young people to participate in the country's development were sought through specific events rooted in their daily lives: a neighbourhood drive, a national campaign or an international event having an impact on the lives of the children or their families.

There was, for instance, a friend, a Ministry of Social Action employee, who invited the young people to participate in the solidarity fund drive to mobilize the entire population in support of victims of the drought, which had been particularly severe in the northern Sahel during the previous winter. The young people's first reaction was to situate themselves among the needy. They argued that, because they were poor, this drive was of no concern to them. But then they realized that the families of several of their own were at risk.

The amount collected was modest, but it represented a genuine contribution on the part of individuals who had never before been approached for such a purpose. On learning of their participation, the Minister of Family Development and National Solidarity decided to meet at length with the children and young people at the former National Assembly building.

This first meeting with a minister was reported in the press and brought the young people an invitation to participate in another campaign launched during the same period, the 'battle of the railway'. Its objective was to enlist the nation's vital forces in building a railway line to link the capital to several towns in the north of the country. Many young people of all ages accepted the invitation, and they went at it with all their strength. The national daily *Sidwaya* ran the following headline: 'Lumpen Proletariat Tackling Railway Battle!' Unfortunately, though, this drive did not bring them into contact with other young people.

Yet another event illustrated the children's need for recognition and participation. At the time of Fespaco 1989,[11] many of them expressed concern at the prospect of the security measures generally deployed on such occasions. As proof of their desire to take part in the preparations for the Festival (which would affect them in many ways), the children were invited to contribute to its success. Following the suggestion of a member of the Festival organizing committee (and a friend of the children), the children were entrusted with cleaning the courtyard of the 'People's House', the centre of political and cultural life in Burkina Faso, where some of the events were to take place. It took intense effort to convince the children that this unpaid labour would alter their image as 'delinquents'.

---

11. Ouagadougou Pan-African Film Festival.

From then on, the Fespaco organizers agreed to support a plan for the young people to use a space next to the stands to set up and oversee a children's game area featuring jigsaw puzzles about African cinema. These puzzles had been made by children participating in Courtyard of a Hundred Trades workshops. Impressed by the children's enthusiasm, the Minister of Social Welfare spread the word. Cultural and film celebrities came to meet with the children in the Courtyard.

There have been many other comparable events over the course of time, by which, with the help of various friends, the children have been able to demonstrate their worth. However, above and beyond getting the children to participate in an empowering initiative likely to benefit others, the main effect of these events was to put the children into contact with people from all walks of life who, impressed with the youths' efforts and moved by their will to serve the community, would then encourage them to persevere for the greater benefit not just of children in difficulties but of society at large. And, with every encounter of this type, a step forward was made.

The meaning of the workshops evolves

Through the health care programme, the young people had reached out to those worse off than themselves. Various events had illustrated their determination to make a contribution to their country's needs. However, it remained for the children to demonstrate even more strongly their resolve to become true partners in the development process. The toy-making workshop was the focus of such a shift.

From 1985 on, the State had begun to pay increasing attention to early childhood development, and this area became a priority for the Ministry of Family Development and National Solidarity. The newly constructed day-care centres were in tremendous need of pedagogical equipment. Meanwhile the team was meeting children between 8 and 12 years of age living on the streets. Their age made them unlikely to join the traditional workshops of apprenticeship to a trade that had hitherto been organized in the Courtyard. Seeking a trade or vocational training was indeed not central to their concerns.

This is how a project to design and make toys for the day-care centres came to be organized in the Courtyard of a Hundred Trades with support from early childhood development specialists. The project carried an important message, namely that children who, for the most part, had never gone to school, and who bore the often heavy burden of a bad reputation, were capable of making toys to develop the intelligence and skills of their younger brothers and sisters. As a result, a more permanent toy-making workshop was set up starting in 1986.

The first order was received in December 1990, and the toys were presented to a day-care centre at a very official ceremony. The press gave the ceremony broad coverage, quoting the words on the banner that had been made for the occasion: "Children Participating in Their Country's Development." For the Courtyard children, this direct encounter with other children and the staff of the day-care centre had a big impact. The entire event served to make them aware of the importance of the work they had done, as reflected in these words used by the principal to introduce them to the little children: "You don't know these big brothers. They don't know you either, but they love you. They sent you toys to play with: toys they made with their own hands. Now they have come to meet you and to see whether you will use them well."

Other orders for toys came in from various sources, including three Recovery and Nutritional Education Centres (Centres de récupération et d'éducation nutritionnelle—CRENs) and a centre for disabled children. Each time, the visits to the centres to present the toys were powerful experiences that recognized the full meaning of the work performed by the youths. The children often came away deeply moved by the encounters they made on these occasions.

Orders placed with other Courtyard of a Hundred Trades workshops became increasingly emblematic of this effort to work as partners in development: a UNICEF order for sewing kits to hold the materials of the Expanded Programme on Immunization teams; a French anti-hunger committee (Comité français contre la faim) request for looms for a village association; a request from a religious community for the construction of small houses for families in great need because of eviction. It was, however, imperative for these orders to remain very limited in number and flexible in the matter of production deadlines, so that training could continue to focus on welcoming children in difficulty.

Participation of the children in the country's cultural development

The toy-making workshop also provided another opening for the young people: an opening onto the world of culture. Spurred by the toy-making workshop's progress and by encouragement from the Ministry of Social Action, the team decided to try its luck in the toy competition held in Bobo-Dioulasso during National Culture Week 1990.

During this week, they ran workshops in different parts of the city as a way to share their knowledge with other children. Many visitors stopped at the Courtyard children's stalls to encourage them, ask them questions and watch them work, and this was a source of pride for the workshop. The award of the fourth and fifth prizes to children from the Courtyard was also a source of pride for all the representatives of their Kadiogo Province.

Weight of insecurity

It was important for us to remain realistic in predicting the extent to which young people who were familiar with the Courtyard would reach out to those in greater need. Although outreach could never be taken for granted, gradual progress was made over the course of time. The highest rate of success was registered in the area of health care, where the children and young people made a very big effort. In 1991, 65 per cent of the newcomers to the Courtyard had come as a result of the health programme. All of them had been either sent to the Courtyard, or accompanied there, by another child.

Another, less obvious, but nevertheless important, aspect of this progress was noted among the older participants, who became increasingly aware of their responsibility towards the younger ones. On several occasions, young people went out and encouraged children to join a workshop even in cases were they themselves were not able to participate. In addition, well before the health care seminar was held, some were volunteering to assist the Courtyard health care team.

We should also emphasize that some children who had a long connection with the Courtyard but whose circumstances remained very insecure had trouble pulling away to make room in the Courtyard for younger children. Even though the Courtyard no longer met their needs, these young people clung to it desperately—it was their lifeline. Their family situation, at times unknown to the team, was an open wound that they found difficult to touch. While all the children suffered similar pain, it could become 'explosive' at times. Perhaps there should be some sort of ritual to encourage a gentle transition, without completely cutting all contacts.

Another observation concerns participation in the country's development, which did not come entirely at the young people's request. Their precarious circumstances did little to encourage a collective effort that would make very little difference to their daily lives. But, buoyed by their confidence in the lasting nature of their relationships with the friends and volunteers, they invested a great deal of energy in such efforts (more than in training activities, which they often viewed as making up for delinquent behaviour) in the hope of achieving greater social recognition. There was no doubt that activities of this type contributed greatly to changing society's perception of them.

3. A partnership for children living on the streets

Partnership with Burkina Faso

From the beginning, contacts were initiated with Burkina Faso through the Ministry of Family Development and National Solidarity. In 1984, a ministry official began participating in meetings held by the friends of the Courtyard in an attempt to build a partnership with the children living on the streets. The approach used by the International Movement ATD Fourth World was consistent with the State's desire: "rather than providing for people, to support them so that they take responsibility for themselves, and each person contributes to national development." In March 1986, an agreement was signed between Burkina Faso and the International Movement ATD Fourth World. This sign of trust encouraged the team to forge ahead in its chosen direction.

A mutual commitment towards collaboration

From then on, regular meetings were held with ministry representatives, and in particular with the heads of the Directorate of Social Reintegration and of the Provincial Directorate of Social Action and the Family. These meetings allowed the State to monitor the project's progress. They were supplemented by an annual activity report. The staff of these directorates often got involved above and beyond the call of duty.

Thanks to the amount of trust accumulated by these frequent exchanges, the team received the backing of the State when needed, e.g., in obtaining funding from an international organization, or in organizing public events or being granted permission to use certain facilities. For its part, the team did all that it could, given its size, to highlight the State's efforts in favour of the young people in greatest need.

In adopting this position, the volunteers had two goals in mind:

- To support the efforts of the Ministries to make an appreciable improvement in the living conditions of children living on the streets, despite very limited resources. Under pressure from the public to 'do something about delinquency', the challenge was to find a way to develop a programme that would avoid further marginalizing these young people or targeting only the most deserving.

- To make every effort to encourage the participation of government employees in the various events in which the children were involved. The objective was not for the State to take over the Courtyard or to replicate this specific experiment by a non-governmental organization with its own identity and strengths, but for the State to discover the potential of these young people once they were enlisted as partners and participants in development, and once they were treated with respect and supported in their endeavours, in particular in their aspirations to re-establish ties with their families in a creditable way.

Sharing experiences

A few years into the experiment of the Courtyard of a Hundred Trades, the approach used there was fully accepted even if it was not entirely consistent with the objectives of the State, which hoped to open other centres throughout the country that, unlike the Courtyard, would be run on conventional lines. At that time, in terms of support for young 'delinquents', the only facilities available were one state-run centre and three private centres.

In 1989, the Secretary of State for Social Action and the Family set up several mechanisms to facilitate the sharing of experiences. By 1990, he began sending social educators and specialized educators to follow training courses of one to three months at the Courtyard of a Hundred Trades. In turn, ATD Fourth World volunteers were invited to participate in the annual meetings of directors of educational centres that were instituted in 1991. The volunteers likewise took part in the 1989-1991 phase of dialogue between the State and donors, which led to the definition of the orientations of the AEMO (Open Education Programme) project. In 1992, the team held a three-month training course for the social educators that had been designated for the AEMO project. The goal was to acquaint them with the children, to introduce them to the services facilitated by the Courtyard and to familiarize them with the approach as experienced on a day-to-day basis. It was a matter of sharing the know-how accumulated over the course of some 10 years of working with the young people.

From the start-up of the AEMO project, a collaboration was established in the field to assist the educators. In addition to monitoring the children living on the streets and their relations with their families, a health care unit was set up at their headquarters. In order to avoid instituting multiple programmes and ensure a greater coordination with the medical services, the educators agreed in July 1993 to take over the Courtyard's eight-year-old health programme. A volunteer who was a medical doctor worked with AEMO for several months to facilitate this transition, including fund-raising efforts (in particular for medicines) for this government initiative.

On the whole, collaboration with the State was extremely positive. First, it allowed the International Movement ATD Fourth World to develop its approach with due regard to the government's wishes. Second, it gave the Ministry of Social Action's services access to a different approach to young people on the streets and their families, defined in the AEMO project, which gave them new hope.

A question remained however as to the formulation of long-term objectives. The educators tended to include the Courtyard of a Hundred Trades among the permanent programmes to which they could direct the young people, whereas ATD Fourth World saw the Courtyard as an evolving 'pilot project', not a permanent programme. While the project was aimed at reversing the negative image of the children and young people as antisocial and revealing their capabilities as partners, its long-term goal was to reunite them with their extremely poverty-stricken families in a manner that displayed respect for the communities.

Partnership with UNICEF

Following a meeting in 1984 between Father Joseph Wresinski and James P. Grant, then Executive Director of UNICEF, the latter expressed the desire to meet with the International Movement ATD Fourth World team in the field during one of his visits to Burkina Faso. Believing that big projects affect the majority, but that it was also important to seek out the people not included in the big programmes, Mr. Grant reasoned that the Courtyard of a Hundred Trades project could yield information on the plight of children living on the streets in Africa and thus make it possible to institute programmes to prevent their numbers from growing.

This meeting resulted in a collaboration with the local UNICEF representatives, featuring an initial period of orientation, from 1985 to 1990. Among its many facets, this collaboration provided tools for the workshops and procured vehicles (a car and a moped) for the use of the volunteers. In a different sphere, the Movement was asked to co-author a UNICEF-funded book, *Children Lead the Way in Burkina Faso.* By describing the experiences of a public day-care centre in a village, ATD Fourth World was honoured to be given an opportunity to lend assistance to the State in fostering early childhood development.

It was not until 1991, however, and the start of the State's AEMO project, subsidized for the most part by UNICEF, that UNICEF support went beyond endorsing the occasional project. UNICEF included the Courtyard of a Hundred Trades in its subsequent five-year plan.

A final comment: While UNICEF frequently cited the Courtyard as an example and directed people to visit it, the volunteers had difficulty making UNICEF understand their wish to maintain flexibility in their plans so as to be able to adapt to the children's lives and remain open to their needs beyond the confines of the Courtyard.

Supporting society's commitment to its neediest members

We considered it essential to target not only the young people but also the community as a whole. This goal was accomplished by the following means:

- Providing opportunities for the children to prove their worth and change society's perception of them by enabling them to speak out in public or to take meaningful action;
- Affording a wide range of people an opportunity to meet personally with the young people on a mutually beneficial basis. For example, working with reporters to produce stories that deal not only with the children's lives but also with their aspirations and the ways in which they participated in various campaigns;
- Suggesting concrete ways that people who wish to lend support to these young people can do so, based on mutual exchange. For example, a suggestion to introduce the young people to sports with a view to providing not just amusement but serious training;
- Widely sharing the experiences of the Courtyard of a Hundred Trades with academics, government officials, local associations wishing to work with children living on the streets, or any other persons or groups moved to action by these children's lives.

Changing society's perceptions

Very often, the young people expressed a strong desire to describe their efforts and make people understand their lives. At the time of Fespaco 1991, one of them enquired: "Couldn't you ask the Fespaco organizers to show the film about the Courtyard so that people will know about the Courtyard and also know how hard we are trying?" At this same festival, with the technical support of a theatre company, they put on a skit called "I Didn't Choose This Life," in which they spoke of their lives and explained the factors that had led them to live on the streets.

In 1987, an event took place that had a big impact on the children's image. The International Movement ATD Fourth World was celebrating its 30th anniversary, and the Courtyard of a Hundred Trades had organized a party to which a variety of partners had been invited, including ministers, representatives of international organizations, aid and NGO officials, various celebrities and friends, relatives of Courtyard children, and reporters. Children from the country's various re-education centres had been invited to participate actively in the event. Two thousand people gathered at the 'People's House' that evening in response to this appeal.

Speaking on behalf of their comrades living on the streets, the children delivered a message that they had prepared with volunteers and friends in one-on-one discussions or in small groups. Together with delegates from other centres in the country, they also performed a skit based on a tale written with two volunteers, entitled 'And We Looked for Tortoise'. Drawn from African traditions, this tale was directly inspired by their lives. It portrayed their distress at feeling rejected and their hope of rejoining their community.

The press played a very important role in changing public opinion. Several television reports presented the children in a positive light on the occasion of various events or activities, including a meeting with the Minister of Family Development and National Solidarity, celebrity visits to the Courtyard of a Hundred Trades, the presentation of toys made by the workshop to a day nursery, a theatre workshop and a health care training seminar.

Making friends, one by one

As was emphasized above, in their dealings with the children the volunteers and friends sought whenever possible to encourage the re-establishment of family ties by affirming their irreplaceable role in the children's future and development.

Great care was put into developing relationships that would break down the isolation and shame that weighed on the children, and enable them to open up to other young people as well as other adults. The idea behind bringing the children into contact with others stemmed from a desire both to provide the children with knowledge by acquainting them with the world around them, and to reveal them to other people, from civil servants to the person in the street, in a new light.

During Fespaco, for example, film directors were invited to the Courtyard to talk about their films with the children. A wide range of other people were contacted, including the Director of the Institut des Peuples Noirs (Institute of Black Peoples), theatre companies, various merchants and school principals. During the health care seminar, visits were organized to places such as the firehouse, laboratories, dispensaries and different departments of the hospital.

With every encounter, something changed in the people who met with the children. A fireman remarked: "We were really surprised. We didn't think that the children would be so interested. They kept on asking questions, including very relevant ones. It was very interesting. The other day, one of them came over to greet me in a bar in Dapoya. I didn't recognize him, but he told me who he was. Don't hesitate; the next time you need us, we'll be there!" A laboratory worker commented: "These children are sharp!" One of his co-workers added: "These children are Burkina Faso's children. We have to look out for them. No one else is going to do it for us."

Following these meetings, several people indicated that they were ready to do more, such as this Red Cross worker: "I often see the children in town, and we chat. They ask me to explain more things. Since it's our role too to advise them, I would like to come and see them at your place. We'll talk things over."

The commitment factor in activities with the children

It was very important to encourage the citizens of Burkina Faso to participate in activities with the children. The most obvious example was that of the artisans. Each time a new workshop was organized in the Courtyard, the team endeavoured to bring in a new artisan selected on the basis of vocational skills and teaching abilities. Since the start of the Courtyard of a Hundred Trades, some 80 artisans had taught training courses. Some of them took on young people as apprentices in their own shops at the end of these courses.

The volunteers encouraged the artisans to go further in their relations with the children. For example, they would invite them to come into the city to visit the children, or to go with a child to see his family. They also spurred them to share their experiences more widely among themselves and with the friends. These steps helped to strengthen the artisans' ties with the children and involved them more and more intimately with the Courtyard. Relationships such as these were very important for the children. In the words of one of them, "The teacher is like an older brother. He shows us everything he knows. He gives us advice." These relationships of trust with adults proved invaluable for the children's future.

Attempts on the part of the volunteers to foster collaboration around the health programme met with less success. They had indeed hoped to establish a permanent relationship with the National School of Health, so that students would come and participate in Courtyard health care and organize meetings to satisfy the children's great need for knowledge on the subject of health. Nothing came of this project, however.

Ties with local associations

In recent years, Burkina Faso has witnessed the emergence of a rather large number of local associations seeking to 'work in favour of the children living on the streets'. Cooperation with these new associations remained for the most part at the stage of establishing contact and discussing Courtyard experiences; a few ties were made that focused on specific situations of children that were known to both groups. It was still too early to engage in joint projects or to entrust specific activities to any of the associations; this was a goal for the future.

In addition, pre-existing movements such as the CV-AV[12] or the Scouts expressed the desire to broaden their activities to include children living on the streets. They invited the International Movement ATD Fourth World to share its experiences at their seminars. On several occasions, leaders in these movements participated in Courtyard activities, specifically in camps for the children. For their part, they invited Courtyard children to attend their camps.

The ties with these youth movements were a source of great hope: hope that a society without borders in which "all hands are useful for transforming the world" could be built through the joint efforts of young people of all backgrounds working side by side, as Father Joseph Wresinski reminded us on the occasion of International Youth Year.

4. Guidelines for action

The aim of this case study has been to describe the different stages of an outreach project targeting children and young people living on the streets under extremely insecure conditions. This particular project worked directly with the children and the appropriate partners in order to elaborate activities based on the young people's expectations, to the greater benefit of the children themselves, their families and their communities. In this final section, we would like to re-emphasize a few key points.

It is clear from all of the above that this kind of approach requires time. No effort must be spared in the attempt to get to know the children living on the streets and, at the same time, to discover the context in which they live, their hopes and their reserves of strength and support. In light of the above, the fact that the person who reached out to them refused to respond immediately to the material requests made of him will appear very significant.

12. Cœurs Vaillants-Ames Vaillantes (Valiant Hearts-Valiant Souls) is a Catholic children's movement.

Over the course of time, it was possible to acquire an in-depth knowledge of the lives of these children and young people. In particular, we found that, of those living on the streets, not all were in the same straits; some were poorer and living in more insecure conditions. The objective was not only to reach these young people as a group, but also to reach each one individually. The initiative also made it clear that the key resided in promoting an activity that would restore their dignity and bring them outside recognition as useful members of society. All of these children and young people were anxious to renew their family ties, regardless of the time that had elapsed since those ties had been severed, which contradicts the generally held view of children living on the streets.

In laying the foundations for action, it was believed necessary to involve on a priority basis those young people who were among the most deprived. The team believed that these young people had to be the starting point and that others would only be able to join if that initial condition had been met. If one begins with the most dynamic, there is nothing to guarantee that a project can be extended to the poorest at a later stage.

The young people were considered true partners on two levels. The first level concerns the role they played in introducing other young people to the Courtyard of a Hundred Trades. The report brings out how they helped each other participate in the programmes, as well as the gestures of solidarity among them. It also indicates the tensions that existed and how it was possible to move beyond them. The second level of partnership concerns the way in which these young people were able to engage in activities that were useful to the country and recognized as such. The toy-making workshop is a good example of this.

Finally, we would like to underline the importance of the ties that were developed and the cooperation that was established between the Movement, the Government of Burkina Faso and local organizations, as well as between the Movement and UNICEF.

THE SAN JACINTO PROJECT

Guatemala: Case study

- Knowing the poorest
- "Our hope is in unity"
- Ensuring the transition
- Guidelines for action

During the 1960s, Father Joseph Wresinski, founder of ATD Fourth World, became acquainted with a group of women calling themselves Caritas, based in the United States. Working with the anti-poverty programmes then under way in that country, the women had committed to an area of the American South plagued by extreme poverty and discrimination. Their approach brought them close to ATD Fourth World, which has remained in touch with them ever since.

In addition to its commitment in the United States, Caritas was also working in Guatemala. During the 1970s, Caritas asked ATD Fourth World to send volunteers to work with them in that region. At that point, the Movement's activities were restricted to the industrialized countries. It was, of course, being urged to consider working in poorer countries also, and the question was under discussion. One evening, during a meeting of Fourth World adults in France, a man got up to say that he had been deeply moved while watching a television report on the plight of families in refugee camps in Asia. He concluded by saying, "Wherever poverty causes so much pain and suffering, there should be volunteers from the Movement."

It was that appeal, and that call to awareness, that led ATD Fourth World to send two volunteers to Guatemala. They arrived in San Jacinto, in the eastern part of the country, on 22 December 1978.

Context

Guatemala, a Central American country, has a population of about 9.5 million.[13] Sixty per cent of the population is rural. These are, of course, estimates. Since 1965-1970, the population has tended to migrate to the cities, mainly to the capital. The country's main resources are agricultural. But while the western and coastal parts of the country are fertile, the land in the east, which has a hot and much drier climate, is arid and unproductive. The municipality of San Jacinto, which at the beginning of the 1980s had about 7,000 inhabitants, lies near the centre of this region. San Jacinto consists of a small central area surrounded by three districts (with about 1,000 inhabitants altogether) along with 11 outlying villages scattered through the surrounding hills.

About half the country's population is indigenous. In some regions, mostly in the west, the people have maintained their traditions, costumes, and languages (more than 20 local languages are still spoken in Guatemala). In the east, the place of origin of the Chorti people, this cultural identity is much less marked. Chorti traditions and the Chorti language survive only in certain villages, and hardly at all in San Jacinto.

Daily life in San Jacinto moves at the same rhythm as agricultural work. Many heads of families own no land, or only a tiny plot. As a result, they cultivate fields belonging to a large landowner and hand over part of the harvest to him. Staple crops are maize and black beans. Although the quality of the harvest varies from year to year, the yield is often inadequate, forcing people to find other resources. In March and April, there are fruit crops (mangoes and *jocotes*). During the dry season, many men and youths make their way towards the coasts, where they find day work on large farms. Families usually keep a few chickens, whose eggs they sell, and they may also have pigs. The women take on simple jobs; the most common is plaiting palm leaves, which they sell to

13. UNDP estimate for 1991. It should be noted that in 1960, the population was estimated at 4 million.

small shopkeepers, who resell them to be made into hats and bags. This type of work is very poorly paid.

It is important to note that the country benefits from a long-standing tradition of community awareness. This is shown in various ways. When a project begins—building a school, laying on water, etc.—a committee is formed. Within the Church (most of the people are Catholic), the communal spirit is expressed through the catechists, lay people who involve themselves in the religious activities of villages and hamlets and also in solidarity initiatives in the communities.

Three additional aspects indicative of recent change should be mentioned.[14]

- Guatemala has been investing in development projects. This has been accomplished in part through the country's own efforts, and in part with international aid. Thus, during the 15 years we spent in San Jacinto, we saw lives improved by a number of small schools being built in the villages and hamlets, several dirt roads being laid to make the communities more accessible, the growth of water supply projects, etc.
- The trend to migrate to the cities. It is generally agreed that there are four reasons for this migration: since the end of the 1960s, an influx towards the various businesses and industries in the capital; in 1976, the earthquake; at the beginning of the 1980s, internal conflicts in the country; and over the past decade, the economic crisis.
- Political changes occurring during the second half of the 1980s, as part of democratization.

Presence of ATD Fourth World

The presence of the Movement team can be divided into three phases: an initial phase, dubbed 'immersion', for the purpose of

14. We wish to touch only *briefly* on these aspects, in order to illustrate the sort of experience on which this document is based, without trying to be all-inclusive. (For example, we do not give figures for illiteracy or mortality.)

getting acquainted; a second phase focusing on programmes carried out in shared responsibility with local partners; and finally a third phase aimed at ensuring a follow-up. In an effort to more accurately describe and illustrate what was undertaken to reach San Jacinto's poorest inhabitants, the following presentation will not follow strictly chronological lines.

1. Knowing the poorest

From the outset, the key question for the team was this: Who are the poorest? We were of course well aware that to reach the stage when this question can be asked takes time. In this chapter, we will make note of a number of steps and events that were important in our effort to become acquainted with the poorest.

Initial stages

The first volunteers arrived to work with Caritas and to learn how to get to know a population. Father Joseph Wresinski had impressed upon us that we needed to allow time for this immersion stage, during which we were to listen and 'internalize'.

Our first job, therefore, was to live in the village and take daily note of what we were learning, which in no way meant remaining mere observers; on the contrary, it required us to share the lives of the people. The fact that we were accompanied by a group already in place for several years made this approach easier, and, as a natural extension of this collaboration, volunteers took an active part in the work of Caritas.

As time passed, and as we met with the people and the people met with the team, team members came to understand the context as described in the Introduction. Although impoverished, the population was capable of coming together to work on projects that held promise for the future, such as the school. The team's attention was soon drawn to two important facts. One was that, even when the general level of energy was high, there were always some people unable to join in. Another fact is that the solidarity we have mentioned is not limited to organized forms, like committees; it can also spring from individual initiatives.

The team thus participated in the Caritas programmes, helping support various committees. At a later stage, team members took on several small-scale projects, such as the production of mango preserves, storing maize in silos, growing soybeans. Through such actions, we were hoping to undertake traditional developmental ventures while at the same time evaluating the role of the very poor, whom we were beginning to know. At the same time, the team involved itself in specific activities to assist extremely poor families (by arranging for children's health care, for example).

Acquaintance based on a committed presence within the community is crucial not only for the initial stages, but also for the duration of the project, in that it affords concrete ways of making progress.

Tools for knowing the poorest

In general, the first requirement of all volunteers, no matter where they are, is to write. In the evening, we would take the time to note down what we had observed and experienced. And we encouraged the Guatemalans working with us to do the same. The Spanish word chosen as a name for our daily reports, *vivencia* (literally, 'what is lived' or 'experience'), acknowledges the fact that, far from considering ourselves outside observers, we record a reality in which we take an active part.

Each week, we met to discuss what we had experienced, what we had discovered, and the lessons we needed to learn if we were to make progress. Indeed, the team's initiatives were continually being questioned in the light of what we were discovering about the people, especially the poorest ones.

Once a month, both at the team level (through a group letter) and at an individual level (through an individual activity report), we would send an account of these matters to the Movement's general secretariat, thus setting up a constructive dialogue with that body.

Meeting the people and getting to know them (and the demands of writing the reports), and making a commitment to the population—none of this happens without moments of doubt and questioning, hence the importance of feeling supported by the team. We shall briefly describe the quarters that served as our team room in San Jacinto. There was a large table, around which we all could sit during meetings, and where we also sat while writing. That room was extremely important to us. It became emblematic, not only for the foreign volunteers but also for the Guatemalans working with us, of the efforts we were making to achieve a deeper knowledge of the poorest, some of whom became members of our permanent Volunteer Corps.

Commitment to the community

Our aim was to be able to work together with the poorest. But in the context of San Jacinto, we could not forgo a broader commitment to the community at large. In a village where poverty is widespread and where, in addition, the first volunteers were foreigners, our only course was to become involved with the entire population. It would have been impossible to get to know the poorest without getting to know the community as a whole.

When most people are struggling to secure such essentials as a school, safe water and good health, talk of the poorest makes little sense. Taking into account the struggle of the entire community and joining them in it were among our top priorities. And the measure of our success in doing so afforded us the opportunity to reflect on the ways in which projects would benefit each and every member of the community, including the most disadvantaged. Conditions were in place for a genuine effort focusing on the poorest, thus avoiding an artificial initiative, imposed from the outside.

Later we would work in the capital, and our approach there would be somewhat different, to the extent that, from the start, we would seek out the very poorest areas.

Human solidarity

In the process of getting acquainted with the population, the team soon encountered men and women who cared deeply about the most disadvantaged. Without any special resources, they were doing their utmost to ensure that the most impoverished members of their community would not be completely abandoned.

We chose to let them guide us, to familiarize ourselves with an often overlooked chapter of a people's history, namely its solidarity with its poorest members. Through them, we met people cruelly affected by poverty. They showed us how they shared the maize harvest with those less fortunate. They taught us the respect they felt for these very poor people.

Some of these men and women are catechists or committee members, but not all. They are, for the most part, simply members of the community, often poor themselves. As they got to know the volunteers, they began to identify with this Movement that had been shaped by the lives of the very poor, whose founder himself had been born in circumstances of extreme poverty. A sense of trust began to grow between them and us. They told us what it meant for a poor person to commit to people who are even worse off. They told us that it was sometimes difficult and discouraging, and that they were hoping to find support for their commitment.

As we followed in the footsteps of these men and women in our effort to reach the poorest, our journey also followed the rhythm of our own discoveries. We also went unaccompanied, off the beaten track, to meet a population that tends to live in hiding because of its poverty. We should add that it often turned out that one impoverished family would lead us to another, whose situation was even worse.

Knowledge

We shall now discuss the role of knowledge in our project. It is important to repeat the definition of knowledge given by Father Joseph Wresinski.

Don Andres Ramos (died August 1992)

Don Andres did not want to head a committee, even when urged to do so by a community long familiar with his sound judgement. His small house of clay and straw was no different from the others in his village. But everyone knew where it was, and they knew they could come there and discuss their problems in complete confidence.

A catechist, he was deeply affected by his neighbours' suffering. He tried to find ways to help them cope; and even when he couldn't find a solution, he was always there. We can vouch for his actions—for example, when he brought the men of the village together to build a house for a woman who was homeless and alone with her children. Such an act was part of his daily routine, and it helped change the life of his village.

When Don Andres met Father Joseph Wresinski, who had come to visit San Jacinto, the priest mentioned his early years, marked by extreme poverty. Don Andres spoke of his own suffering and that of his people, and said that two of his children had died in infancy. The two men did not speak the same language. But during the time they spent together, their eyes never left each other and they understood one another perfectly. At the end, they stood up and clasped each other in a long embrace.

When we talked with Don Andres in 1989, he reiterated his concern for the poorest: "I always say to the catechists, we are not the poorest, because we have our speech, our hands, our feet. The poorest are those who cannot walk, who have nothing, who have no roof over their heads.... We must reach out to them and give them something." Then, after a moment of silence, he added, "Our hope is in unity."

When we refer to a cultural project, we mean the need to grant the very poor access to "knowledge", as defined by Father Joseph.[15]

Our experience in San Jacinto taught us that the sharing of knowledge has a vital place in a project whose goal is to reach the poorest.[16] Why is the sharing of knowledge so essential? Because it responds to a basic ideal of the most disadvantaged. Before discussing the role and meaning of sharing knowledge we shall try to describe it briefly. The first knowledge initiative was the 'library in the fields', a programme that is still in effect today. Set up in 1981, the first library was run by a volunteer and two young Guatemalans. They brought books to a relatively isolated hamlet. A few children plucked up the courage to approach them. They gathered around a very simple picture book that dealt with the egg, the hen and the chick, realities the children recognized. The children began to talk and react as they looked at the pictures. Then a mother joined the group. Another book dealt with plants. This started an exchange of ideas on the subject: plants that were familiar to the village people, and the ways they were used. When the library visit was over, the organizers promised to return the following week. On the day, more children joined the original group, and more mothers came to watch. The library was gaining momentum: Children brought more children, and the organizers met other families and invited them to participate.

---

15. *Revue Igloos–Quart Monde,* 'L'enfant du Quart Monde en quête de savoir' (The Fourth World child in search of knowledge), No. 105-106, 2nd trimester 1979.

16. We have observed this all over the world. Everywhere, we saw Father Joseph's actions at the Noisy-le-Grand camp for the homeless repeated. It was a basic initiative: Rejecting the charity of a soup kitchen, he founded instead a kindergarten and a library.

One aspect of the library is that anyone can be a part of it, at any time. It takes place outside, right in the middle of the community. There are no conditions for attending. Families can come and see what it is all about, parents are free to join in. Along with our visits to families, the library helped us to start attracting the poorest. Gradually, we made our way towards the most isolated houses, some of them virtually hidden, and others that were just palm shelters. This hands-on approach helped us to locate hamlets and to meet the poorest families, the ones who generally do not come forward. The active, involved families were with us from the beginning, but we had to make the effort to seek out the others and explain to them what the library was all about before the poorest would join in.

The library can thus be perceived as a medium to meet the poorest and to establish a relationship of trust. However, a library also has its own agenda, which is to grant access to knowledge, the driving force behind community participation. If we look at our definition of knowledge, we see that a library is not just a place to learn. It is more than that: it is there to open a window onto the world, affording an opportunity for dialogue and self-expression. An image comes to mind to explain its reach: A person who lives in poverty is like a bird that has fallen to the bottom of a rain spout; it can no longer fly because it has no room to spread its wings. If it is to fly, the spout enclosing it must be opened. This is the function of the sharing of knowledge: It breaks through the walls of poverty that keep the very poor imprisoned.

Knowledge is not just a window on the world, it is also a key component in establishing a positive identity. In fact, poor people are most often viewed in terms of their shortcomings (illiteracy, high mortality rates, isolation, slum housing, etc.) and not in terms of what they could and do bring to others. Their potential for giving is unsuspected because they have no way to show it. So the rest of the world comes to believe, mistakenly, that they have nothing to offer. The knowledge initiative encourages all of us—*them and us*—to prove the opposite.

The library is not limited to books; we also introduce things like colouring, drawing, singing and various other kinds of artistic expression. This helps the very poor to enrol in other projects such as craft workshops and programmes for development. Knowledge is indeed a prerequisite for achieving development.

We mentioned that the first library was set up with the help of two young Guatemalans. That programme and the one that followed, like the pre-school, were a common effort with the people of the country. This led to a whole social mobilization initiative, to which we will return later.

The poorest

Reaching the poorest is a long journey, requiring an investment in time. As we have said before, we found ourselves face to face with a uniformly poor population. And our concern was with the whole of that population. However, we could never posit that a programme was good simply because it seemed to work or because a large number of people were involved in it. The criterion of success was our ability to reach the poorest, and in the end, it was through them that our efforts would be judged.

Today, with the benefit of hindsight, are we able to identify the poorest? Certainly, but spelling out their defining characteristics is much harder. First, there are the faces that are etched into our memories, the individuals and the families we met, those who, in this context of widespread poverty, seemed to have stumbled, whereas others had stayed on their feet. This way of describing the situation may not seem adequate. We have described the techniques we used to reach the stage of getting to know people. Rather than sociological concepts, it is the individuals met in the field and the experiences that we were afforded that come to mind when we try to describe the poorest. Although they are important in the process of development policies, sociological constructs tend to ignore the human aspect and do not take into account what matters more to us—the actual gestures of solidarity that enter into the fabric of daily life among the poor and the poorest.

We tried to adopt a rigorous approach in our attempt to understand the lives of those we judged to be poorer than the others. Early on, the team's attention was drawn to the situation of women living alone with children. Typically, they live in a state of extreme poverty, and the catechists took special care to call them to our attention. The community often organizes acts of solidarity in favour of such women, bringing them necessities for building a small house. Together with their children, some women are taken in by families that are in better circumstances. In such households, they may perform domestic chores. At times, they and their children may be exploited in such situations, but this is not usually the case.

In this way we became aware, first, that these women find themselves in a variety of predicaments, and then, that acts of solidarity are easier to organize around such women than around very poor families where a man is still present.

We were also interested in men who were obliged to go to work on the coast for part of the year (see Context, page 58). To be forced to relocate in order to find work is clearly a sign of unpredictable living conditions.

But we soon learned that this was not confined to the very poor. We had questions concerning how far people were living from the village centre. The least poor hamlet turned out to be one of the most distant, and for a long time we were unable to reach it. So what was the meaning of this variable, given that some very poor families live in remote, inaccessible areas, often in hiding?

The traditional dwelling is a living space consisting of a single room (sometimes two), with walls of cob and practically no furniture. A family with not even that much—no house, or just a palm shelter—would appear to be living in acute poverty. But once again, circumstances alter cases; in certain areas the earth is suitable for building houses and in others it is not, and there we are more likely to see rudimentary structures made of palm.

A great many people have no land. Also, lack of access to public facilities—health centres, for example—is a fairly common problem. All this led us to decide that a single variable does not permit us to draw conclusions about extreme poverty.

This explains the method we used to get to know the people and become involved with them, while always making the effort to reach the poorest. It also points up the fact that there are no strict lines separating the poor from the very poor. But even if poverty can be charted along a 'continuum', one should never forget that poverty does not touch all the members of a community in the same way.

When living conditions become intolerable, when instability piles up, the people affected lose their grip on their own lives. They have to go out and scrape up the means of survival every day, with no guarantees for the next day. The first and most obvious effect is that they are unable to take part in communal or development projects. This can cause people to say, "They're lazy, they just can't be bothered." But when a man with a family is asked to contribute 50 working days to a water supply project, while his family is allotted a food ration for that period of time,[17] he is in no position to accept if he has to work to pay off debts incurred earlier in the season. He is one of those who have never been able to put money aside. This is a common example, and it shows why the poorest find it difficult to participate in community action.

How, then, are we to understand—to decipher—the attitudes of those families marked by poverty? Let us take the example of the man who came to our house one night, asking for vitamins for his little girl. What was hidden behind his anxious face? How urgent was it to give him

17. This is called *alimentos por trabajo* (food-for-work), a widespread custom. A community project is carried out with the help of the population, who provide the labour, and during the work period, they receive food, most often through the World Food Programme (WFP).

vitamins? It turned out that his 15-month-old daughter was at death's door. And by the time we saw her it was too late; she had become dehydrated from diarrhoea while suffering from severe malnutrition. How were we to react? It was especially important not to say: "Why didn't you come around sooner? If you had only come even 24 hours earlier, something could have been done." To say such things would serve only to add to his guilt, it would have been not only pointless but also extremely unfair. Instead, we had to try to understand how this father had somehow found his way to our house at nightfall, how things were for this family that could not manage to feed the children even though both parents were working, how they were never at peace because there was always a child who was ill. We had to understand their shame at seeing debts piling up endlessly and never being able to join in a community project. We had to walk that road with them so that trust could be established[18] and we could take action together.

2. "Our hope is in unity"

We compare this saying of Don Andres Ramos to a text by Father Joseph Wresinski, which is engraved on a commemmorative stone at the Trocadéro Plaza in Paris: "Wherever men and women are condemned to live in extreme poverty, human rights are violated. To come together to ensure that these rights be respected is our solemn duty."

Towards projects undertaken by the poorest

Finding and getting to know the poorest does not ensure that they will therefore participate in a community project. It is certainly a prerequisite, but a strategy must be put in place that will enable the poorest to become genuine partners. The best way is by granting them full recognition as individuals and as citizens.

18. This idea of trust is essential; we used to say that we 'knew' a family when a relationship of trust had been established between us.

We therefore put a great deal of effort into working with local and community organizations during this initial phase. This was to ensure that both development projects and community initiatives would involve the poorest. The first volunteers wrote, "We are facing a challenge: Is development actually possible without excluding the poorest?" It was to answer that question that we joined the community and the Government in projects such as the water supply, in daily work at the health centre, and so on.

However, reaching the poorest entailed more than enlisting their participation in community projects. It also meant joining them in projects which are extremely important to them precisely because of their great poverty, and which that very poverty prevents them from voicing.

An initiative of ours illustrates this strategy, namely the fight against child malnutrition.

Malnutrition: a reality

In the very poor families we knew in San Jacinto, the life of a child is constantly under attack from disease. The death of small children is a reality that all those families know well. And even if their attitude is somewhat fatalistic, parents nevertheless fight with all their strength to keep their children alive.

Figures[19] are available at the national level that give us a general idea about infant mortality and malnutrition. They indicate

---

19. The mortality rate of children under five: 94 per 1,000 live births (according to UNDP, 1993).

INCAP found that 70 to 75 per cent of children under five in the country were suffering from malnutrition (all stages combined); these figures were quoted by Dr. M. Gehlert in *Vida, enfermedad y muerte en Guatemala* (Life, Illness and Death in Guatemala) (1984).

According to the 1993 UNDP report, 35 per cent of children under five were underweight and 68 percent of children between 24 and 59 months were stunted in growth.

that malnutrition is relatively widespread (although it has been declining over the past 15 years). In regard to severe malnutrition, which constitutes a direct threat to the life of a child, the figures available are less precise.

Without going into technical detail, we can state that severe malnutrition is the end result of a combination of factors. Among them are the mother's health and nutritional status, food supplies, infections and illnesses, living conditions (housing, lack of safe water, etc.), difficulty in reaching health facilities and factors linked to ignorance. These observations are borne out by UNICEF and in *Assignment Children*. In very poor families, all these elements converge to create a truly vicious circle. We observed that the most serious situations, in terms of malnutrition, occurred most often in the poorest families.

Launching the project

A project specifically geared towards fighting child malnutrition was launched in 1984. That initiative took place in the period of 'shared responsibility'.

At that time, we believed that the conditions favourable to such a project were in place. First, the team had built up a thorough knowledge of the community and with the most disadvantaged families. Second, one of the volunteers, a doctor who had been in the field for a year, had put a great deal of work into health facilities (especially the San Jacinto health centre) and into interaction with the population (by visiting the hamlets among other community-oriented activities). Finally, another group[20] was hoping to become involved in such a project and was in a position to contribute human and material aid. The health centre also was in favour of the project.

---

20. Alianza para el Desarrollo Juvenil (Alliance for Youth Development).

However, the manner in which these partners approached the matter gave us some cause for concern. Their entry point was the *comedor* (dining room); they wanted to set up a place where children would receive a balanced diet. This approach seemed problematical to us. The whole history of the Movement warned us against a project that, although it was not limited to distributing food, could easily degenerate into a public-assistance programme. In San Jacinto itself, we had learned from very poor families that they failed to recognize malnutrition as such. They see only a child who is ill, or not growing properly ("he's a year and a half, and he's still not walking"). This sort of talk was common among mothers. These families also made us realize that the project should not be focused on a negative and painful aspect of their lives. Indeed, to take such an approach would work only with the most enterprising members of the community. How would it be viewed by the poorest? How could they see it otherwise than as a reproach, highlighting something that causes them deep suffering?

The three phases of our involvement

There is always something artificial about the division of an event into phases. But it can help in understanding how things evolved. For that reason, to distinguish these phases, we have selected certain striking events that marked the different stages.

1. *Immersion*: This period begins with our arrival in December 1978 and ends with the first 'knowledge month' (December 1982). It is characterized by the desire to meet the population and pave the way for a closer acquaintance. At the same time, the knowledge initiative is set up. Knowledge month is held in several villages (a week of activity in each, with a group of young people from San Jacinto).
2. *Shared responsibility projects*: This phase begins with the first pre-school (in the village of Las Lomas). Following the 1982 knowledge month, the team decides to start a pre-school in

one of the poorest of the areas where the activities had taken place. The pre-school is headed by a Guatemalan woman teacher who recently joined the volunteer corps.

This is the phase during which the team concentrates on programmes carried out with members of the population and other local partners. It ends in May 1989.

3. *Ensuring the transition*: In May 1989, the team moves from San Jacinto to the departmental administrative centre, 20 km away. From here, it continues to support commitments that now are more and more the responsibility of the inhabitants of San Jacinto.

This is where we see once again the importance of sharing the ambitions of the most disadvantaged. We knew that they were capable of a long-term effort for their children's future, so that they would have a normal development. We had seen it in the pre-school that had opened in January 1983. At the beginning of the year, the project had six children (from two families); by the end of 1983, there were 30 children from about 10 families.

Therefore, if we were to participate, we insisted that the child malnutrition project be centred on a pre-school[21] whose direction we agreed to assume. It is on the basis of those terms that a nutritional centre was planned to open end-June 1984, in the village of Lomas.

This project had two main goals:

a) to secure a place in the programme for families with the greatest need, i.e. those whose children were the most severely malnourished;

b) to ensure that the results could be seen, not only in terms of nutritional well-being but also in terms of the development

---

21. Today it is generally agreed that any malnutrition project is more effective when integrated with a programme of early childhood stimulation (as shown by a study in Cali, Colombia).

of psychomotor skills and the child's overall growth. It was also important that those advances be experienced by parents in a way that would benefit the whole family in the longer term.

Partnership with the poorest

At the outset, relatively few of the poorest families took part in the project. Their gradual introduction into the project was made possible precisely because our first concern was to seek them out. Only after a relationship of trust had been established did we suggest participation in the project, a suggestion that was well received because the project was centred on a pre-school. Here is a concrete example: We had met a family whose child was so debilitated by illness and malnutrition that his mother could not imagine taking him out with her. Burdened by shame, suspicion and seemingly endless suffering, she stayed at home. We therefore decided to work directly with her, introducing the methods of the project at her home until the child began to show improvement. At that point, he was able to leave home and join in the project, and the family joined the others in the public centre. This is not an unusual story; on several occasions an initial phase within the family was necessary to ensure subsequent affiliation with the group.

In practical terms, the nutritional centre's programme functioned as follows. Four times a week, the children gathered in a building lent by the hamlet school. The pre-school activities (based on early childhood stimulation techniques) lasted about an hour and a half. We made sure that the mothers (or sometimes an older sister) joined in these activities; in fact, that was a key factor in how the project worked. On a regular basis,[22] the team's physician saw the children at the centre, to treat coexisting ailments and observe each

22. At least once a week, but the frequency varied according to the children's needs and their states of health. In addition to these visits to the centre, the doctor also made house calls.

child's progress. These medical visits were carried out in a place that may not have been completely conventional, but at least a child could be examined in privacy, along with the mother. Everything concerning a child's health, including weight charts, remained in the child's file. This was all done with an eye to maintaining the families' privacy.

Finally, came the preparation of a snack and a meal, adapted to the particular needs of each child. The meals were composed of foods normally available in the region, such as black beans, the highly nutritious component of the corn-bean combination on which the region's diet is based. Young children are not normally given this food. In fact, young children do not easily digest the whole bean, so traditionally they are only given the broth in which the beans are cooked. But children can digest the beans perfectly well if they are puréed, and this was a practice we tried to introduce. In the same way, we showed that eggs are a highly nutritious food, and that it made more sense to give eggs to the children rather than sell them. Not surprisingly, the children's nutritional status also required the addition of a milk-based supplement.

Basing our work on the pre-school and on medical and nutritional monitoring, we were able to turn this project into a comprehensive programme. Once trust had been established within a group that had evolved a cohesive dynamic, it became easier to introduce into community projects a water supply component, which was so important for family health and well-being.

This project was founded on a multiple partnership, starting with the families most affected by poverty. We have described how, from the outset, our interaction with them led us to centre the project on the pre-school. But even later, we continued adjusting and adapting the project according to the families' experiences and suggestions. A partnership also existed with the young people of San Jacinto; some of them who had trained with us in the libraries and other knowledge initiatives helped in coordinating the pre-school. Health workers were actively involved also. Finally, there was a partnership with another non-governmental organization, and, most important of all, with the San Jacinto health centre.

We held regular meetings to discuss how things were going, in effect a kind of continuous evaluation that enabled us to reorganize the programme's structure. We also held training sessions with the young people who were helping coordinate pre-school activities.

Informal evaluation

During 1986, the nutritional centre was moved from the school to a small unoccupied house that had been made available to us. The move was prompted by the need to accommodate more very poor families. And the decision was made by all those concerned.

The Lomas nutritional centre remained in operation for three years, during which time 70 children attended.

It should be mentioned here that in 1985 our experience with the centre led us to set up a similar one in the village of Tizubin. Starting with these pilot projects, a more extensive programme took shape at the health centre.

In July 1987, we decided to discontinue the project at the Lomas nutritional centre, the number of children justifying the need for such a facility having declined considerably. From the nutritional point of view, the children had recovered. In addition, something had changed in the families; the parents were better able to deal with their children's health and nutrition needs. One indication of this was the strengthening of ties between the families and the health centre. Keeping the centre open would have heightened the risk of its being relegated to a public assistance function, because of the food distribution programme. It was time, therefore, to conclude the project, at least in that particular form.

We kept the pre-school going, however. The parents placed great value on it. The pre-school allowed us to carry through the whole project in terms of the young child's overall development. As for those children who still required a nutritional follow-up, we directed them to the health centre, which, as previously mentioned, had instituted a general programme for the community at large.

We cannot say that malnutrition was completely eradicated. Severe poverty still exists, and the threat that hangs over the health of young children has not gone for good. But this project, by putting a comprehensive process at the service of health, enabled very poor families to learn that illness and the death of young children were not inevitable, and that, by working together, people can overcome a great deal.[23]

We have mentioned that the poorest families did not join in at the beginning. We have explained how they entered the project gradually and ended up playing a major role. In the village of Lomas, with no more than a thousand inhabitants, we managed to get to know all the families. We are therefore in a position to state that the poorest among them did indeed make a positive contribution.

Having followed the different stages of this programme, we believe it has had beneficial effects on the whole community, because of the important investment of all parties, including that part of the community most directly concerned.

---

23. It may appear surprising that evaluation figures are not quoted here. They could have been based, for example, on data available at the health centre concerning infant mortality or on medical consultations concerning malnutrition. We do not quote them because they are difficult to interpret. And although they show an improvement in the situation of the entire community of San Jacinto, this was the end result of a combination of efforts. Within that combination, this project is but one contribution, which is special because it was carried out among the most disadvantaged.

The story of Doña Maria's family

When the nutritional centre opened, we barely knew Doña Maria, and no one thought to invite her. Her family lived virtually in hiding. One of her sons had come to the library in the fields on occasion, but we did not know the family.

One day around the end of July 1984, Doña Maria came to the clinic at the centre. A neighbour who had joined the project told her: "Go see the doctor, it isn't far...and your boy is so ill." She hesitated, but finally she came. It was sad to see her there, looking so awkward, so fearful, so worried. In her arms Doña Maria held Juventino, a 15-month-old boy who was in a very bad way. She hardly dared utter a word. Juventino was severely malnourished, and he had bronchopneumonia. He was given treatment, and the team doctor offered to go see him the next day at home. The mother accepted. The following day, a neighbour whom we knew showed us the way to Doña Maria's house. It was not so much a house as a pitiful shelter made of branches and a few pieces of wood on which palm leaves and pieces of plastic had been placed. It was buried in the undergrowth. The family had only a few square metres of land, but the father, Don Luis, had planted some corn. No poor family can afford to lose an inch of land where something will grow to help feed them.... To earn a living, he works for a landowner, on a rocky piece of terrain in the heights around the village, a long way from where he lives. He works under the traditional system, which means he gives the owner part of the harvest. Doña Maria and her eldest daughter, Xiomara, age 16, plait palm leaves, which they sell to a trader who comes through the village.

Several visits were needed to track the child's progress. Trust began to grow. And little by little, Doña Maria was able to tell us her story. She had given birth to ten children, but four died in infancy. "Two died of oedema," she says. When parents speak of this symptom, which they have watched strike and carry off their children, we understand that death was due to malnutrition. With the first child, she went to the health centre, where she was told there was no medication for the condition. For Doña Maria, to walk to the health centre and back with a child in her arms takes three and a half hours. The experience made her believe that to go to the health centre was useless, that when faced with illness there was nothing you could do. The third child died of measles, she says. And the fourth, of diarrhoea. Speaking with great emotion, she continued: "For several days, he couldn't keep anything down, he vomited everything, he had diarrhoea. My husband was working in the fields, and I had to take him tortillas. It was a long walk...I didn't dare leave the baby at home. So I took him on my back and went out to carry the food. On the way, I realized the diarrhoea hadn't stopped. When I came back, he was dying. He was 10 months old."

Naturally, we suggested to Doña Maria that she come to the nutritional centre with Juventino and Catalina, her three-and-a-half-year-old daughter. She discussed it with her husband. They were unsure. They were afraid to mix with the others, and undoubtedly ashamed of their children's state of health. A neighbour supported our suggestion: "Listen, I go there too. I can see that it's doing my kids good." So then the parents decided that Juventino and Catalina would go. At first, it was hard for them, and they came only irregularly. It was the neighbour who brought the children. Doña Maria would come only when she wanted to see the doctor with one of her children.

But we always kept up the contact with the family, going to visit them at home. Actually, Doña Maria almost never left her house, and then only to take the tortillas to her husband in the fields, or on rare occasions when she came down to the village centre. But she wanted her children to stay in the project. So the family decided that Xiomara, the older sister, would go with the two younger ones. Little by little, the two began to benefit from the activities; we could see them making progress in the pre-school; they participated more and more, became more cheerful; and the learning process was accelerating. Xiomara also got fully involved in the project. Like the mothers, she prepared a meal for the group once a week; she helped her brother and sister hold their pencils for colouring and guided them in the early childhood stimulation exercises. And when these things were reported back to Doña Maria, her face would break into a broad smile. She was proud of her children.

From that point on, the family was gradually able to resume contact with the health centre, first by coming to the immunization drive, then by having the courage to come back for treatment. In 1985, Doña Maria gave birth to a little girl, Flora.The family was able to use what it had learned in the project to help Flora. The moment Flora fell ill, her mother came to seek treatment. And Flora has never suffered from malnutrition.

In December 1985, Don Luis brought his children to the festivities of knowledge month, in the San Jacinto square. To mark an end to the month's activities, we had organized workshops and a show. In one of the workshops, Don Luis and his children worked together to make a little crèche (it was just before Christmas), which they took back to the village to decorate their home. At the end of 1987, Don Luis was able, with the help of neighbours, to rebuild his house.

3. Ensuring the transition

At the present time, we have acquired a perspective that allows us to examine the long-term prospects for our work with a very disadvantaged group. The departure of the team from San Jacinto can provide us with material for discussion.

Leaving San Jacinto

Most of the initiatives we undertook were carried out in partnership with others. We have made that clear. Projects such as the nutritional centre or the work dealing with health were from the start carried out in partnership with national groups or using existing infrastructure. The knowledge initiative was accomplished with the help of young people. The embroidery workshop was started by the team, then taken over by a Guatemalan national agency.

We wanted the poorest to be partners in these initiatives. With the achievement of that partnership, it constituted an experience that became part of the history and the memory not only of the poorest, but also of the whole community.

In 1989, the team's commitment in the country broadened; by then, part of the team was working in the capital. The volunteers in San Jacinto, after due discussion with the Movement as a whole and with our partners in the region, decided to settle in the administrative centre of the department (Chiquimula), some 20 km from the centre of San Jacinto. One reason for this move was to physically distance ourselves from San Jacinto, to allow the local people to take over more of the responsibility, while remaining close enough to provide any necessary help.

At that point, we cut down our operations and our programmes, while maintaining a presence to ensure future progress and to make sure that the poorest continued to play active roles in their community. This transition was made possible by several individuals and groups: a group of young people, some friends working in the area and eager to discuss things with us, among them a teacher from one of the villages. There were also the Guatemalan organizations, like the institution that took over the embroidery workshop or the health centre. (The health technician retained close ties with us.) There were, of course, the members of the community mentioned earlier who were committed to working with the poorest before our arrival. Finally, there were those among the very poor who had experienced such momentous changes in their lives that they wanted to share them with others. That was what happened with the man whom we described in the section on knowledge (who came to ask for vitamins when his daughter was dying).[24] He became involved in a small farming project with a Guatemalan volunteer, and when the volunteer left, the man was able to continue.

The youth group

Caritas had already organized a group of young girls. So from the beginning we had been in touch with San Jacinto's young people. They came to play an important part in many of our projects, particularly those centred on knowledge initiatives.

Who are these young people? Our first contact was with youngsters from humble backgrounds who wanted to work together and were eager to help people worse off than themselves. The group grew rapidly, bringing in youngsters from very poor families, and also some from families that were better off and living in the centre of the community. This was not just a group of young people leading an initiative; it was the birth of a young people's movement.

Wanting them to succeed, we paid close attention to every aspect of the activities they were involved in (preparatory and evaluation meetings, training sessions, urging them also to write reports). Responding to their thirst for knowledge, we then tried to give them opportunities to educate themselves (support for schooling, technical training, etc.) A substantial investment was required in order to work side by side with the young people.

Among the initiatives that are still in operation today, one is especially meaningful. We are referring to the knowledge

---

24. See pages 69–70.

campaigns. Several times a year, young people go to secluded hamlets in order to lead a week of library activities and workshops. Young people with secondary school training take charge of these activities. Each group is accompanied by an older youth who is already well trained in this type of library work. In addition, the school's headmaster and a teacher handle the supervision and coordination of these campaigns. The campaigns conclude with the knowledge month, which takes place during the school vacation. The last knowledge month (1993) was organized and led entirely by young people, without the help of volunteers.

This process of sharing knowledge is crucial to all concerned. Rosa, a young woman from San Jacinto and a volunteer in the Movement, had been working in Honduras. When she returned to San Jacinto for a holiday, she met Carmen's father. These people belonged to a relatively well-off family living near the centre of the village. Carmen participated in the knowledge month. Rosa reports: "Carmen's father was pleased with what his daughter had accomplished, with what she had found out in going to hamlets she hadn't known before. And she herself was impressed by what she had seen, too. Her father told her, "You see, Carmen, we don't have anything to complain about. Now you know how some people live over there in the hidden corners of your village." Rosa adds, "For me, this is full of hope."

4. Guidelines for action

As we near the conclusion of this case study, we can attempt to learn some lessons concerning partnership with the poorest. What are the terms of such a partnership?

Two elements seem to us to be fundamental: understanding and time.

- Arriving at a thorough understanding of what the poorest go through seems vital to us. It is thus essential to find the means to achieve such an understanding, and we have described those tools with which we experimented. This is a genuine training component and is crucial to any commitment to work alongside the most disadvantaged.

- A willingness to invest time is another prerequisite. Linked to the first insofar as understanding requires time, this is also a condition in and of itself, to allow the poorest to participate.

Both the time and the understanding factors therefore constitute two key elements in ensuring that a proposed initiative meet the deepest ambitions of the very poor, ambitions they are not readily able to articulate.

An initiative must strive to be comprehensive, for poverty has repercussions on every aspect of life. No single initiative is sufficient, of course, to affect every aspect of life at once; any initiative must, nonetheless, take into account reality as experienced in its entirety, and must contribute to significantly improving the quality of life of the very poor.

An initiative must aim to restore dignity to very poor families. By its connection with the pre-school, as we have said, the nutritional centre offered a positive outlook to the most disadvantaged families. They were invited to work together towards a goal they could recognize as theirs: the well-being of their children. Any reference to malnutrition, a painful and negative aspect of their lives, was downplayed.

The sharing of knowledge played a key role, in our San Jacinto experience, in enabling the poorest to become partners.

In the context of that poor rural community, a commitment to the most disadvantaged had to be based on a pact with the entire community. The pact was essential both to the progress of the project and to inspire the mobilization of energy needed. This mobilization was sustained after the volunteers left.

The various aspects discussed above were key factors in fostering the participation of those among the poorest who aspired to contribute to the well-being of their community.

THE FONDS-DES-NÈGRES PROJECT

Haiti: Case study

- Library in the fields
- Educational initiative

In 1977, a Catholic priest serving the parish of Saint Joseph in Pemel, the principal town, started a small boarding school to accommodate around 60 girls. These girls came from very poor families and, without this initiative, would have had no chance of attending school, especially since some were already 14 years old. In the course of a year or two, they received a basic education designed to enable them to 'manage' in life. In November 1981, the priest asked the International Movement ATD Fourth World if it could send permanent volunteers to help him develop this school following the death of its headmistress. It was in this context that three women volunteers from the Movement came to Fonds-des-Nègres.

Fonds-des-Nègres is a rural community of 40,000 located in southern Haiti, 120 km from Port-au-Prince, the capital. Most Haitians are peasant farmers. In Fonds-des-Nègres, as in the rest of the country, farm families are poor. Families without land, families headed by mothers and families in which fathers are forced to go elsewhere to seek work as day labourers are poorer still. In many instances, their children suffer from malnutrition. What is more, in the most distant reaches of the *mornes* (hills), the most enterprising of the people have left. Those who remain lead a very hard life and are cut off from everything. Some are so poor that they are excluded from the rest of society.

Children from these very poor families generally have no access to schooling. Their parents do not make enough money to cover the expenses associated with school. Furthermore, school discipline requires children to be diligent, punctual and clean, and in certain cases, to wear a uniform. Lastly, school enrolment takes place at the age of six or seven, by which time very poor children are obliged to perform simple tasks to assist their families: helping in the fields, selling at the market or working as domestic help. However, even if a fraction of the population still receives no schooling, the country is doing its utmost to make education available to all children. So high are the stakes of education, in that it provides prospects for a future, that all families are eager to secure schooling for their offspring. A few free schools have been opened here and there, including in the *mornes.* It is not uncommon to see schools that are attached to parishes (parochial schools).

Origin of a project

The three volunteers were not, strictly speaking, just teachers. They had as their background and point of reference their experience with the International Movement ATD Fourth World. Their first human priority was to meet with Fonds-des-Nègres' poor families, especially its most isolated and excluded ones, so that they would be able to take these families' ambitions for their children's future into account. This absolute determination to make personal contact with the families of the rural community of Fonds-des-Nègres and to elicit their views as to what needed to be done was inspired both by the ATD Fourth World's approach and by the analysis of the situation described above.

From the analysis, it was fairly apparent that ignorance, the scourge of the poorest for generations, could not be fought solely on the basis of the existing school system, which served only the relatively privileged children in this rural area: those from families whose resources provided a minimum degree of security or who lived closest to the school. It failed to reach the children from the most isolated and poorest families—the ones, as it happened, that needed their children to work in order to survive. For this reason, it was important from Day 1 not to become locked into merely providing teaching assistance and management for the existing school, even if the Pemel school represented a very positive effort.

Rather, to reach the poorest, we would have to form a special partnership through which the parents' wishes for their children's education, the young people's need to be useful to others and the children's hunger for knowledge could produce results that would be tangible to them.

Reaching out to the poorest families: Library in the fields

During their first few months, the volunteers noted that many of the boarders at the Pemel school came from Guirand, an isolated locality in the *mornes,* and that these girls were having great difficulty keeping up in class. It was thus very natural for the volunteers to start with this locality in their effort to become acquainted with the children's everyday environment, establish contact with the parents and meet with other families.

In February 1982, they began organizing a 'library in the fields' there every Saturday morning. Very soon, a young Haitian woman from Guirand came to help them. This library initiative was perceived as the sign of an investment in human effort, and as such, aroused interest because it tried to respond to what the community wanted. This new activity became a magnet for the neighbourhood; children and adults came to look at the books and took an interest in what could be learned from them. After a few weeks, however, the volunteers noticed that some Guirand children were not coming to the outdoor library activities, either because they were busy working at home or in the fields or because they were too ashamed of their clothes to join with the other children.

In this case, the library had to be brought to those children, making it mobile, following the paths that the children took from the fields or the river and even going to their homes, where attractive books could be shown to the entire household. Gradually, completely isolated children who would not have come to the outdoor library on their own began to appear, displaying a desire for discovery and learning that no one would have suspected, not even their own families.

This effort to reach out to the most isolated and excluded families, the simplicity of the means deployed, the energy generated around the picture books as they were read out loud and discussed by the audience—all of this sparked growing interest and a desire to participate among the young men and women of Fonds-des-Nègres. This budding commitment on the part of highly motivated young Haitians called for support. We needed to provide them with training that would enable them to organize their own sessions around books, stories and songs. We also had to encourage them in their resolve to bring in the most isolated and excluded people.

By the summer of 1982, outdoor libraries were organized in other areas of Fonds-des-Nègres, specifically in Jovange and in Pemel itself. Later on, more libraries, in Viaux and in Pélissier for example, were started at the request of the young people, who were anxious to reach the most isolated and neglected groups. Wherever they were set up, the libraries sparked children's interest in learning and opening up to the world around them and afforded young people an opportunity to make a commitment. They also offered parents the prospect of a greater solidarity and inspired hope for a school that would accept their children, no matter how far behind they were or what difficulties they had, and in which they, the parents, could participate more fully.

Educational initiative gets a second wind

Encouraged by the level of community interest and the energy it mobilized, the volunteers took stock of the hopes and efforts of Haitian society in the area of education. They helped facilitate changes in the Pemel school that were geared towards fostering greater participation by poor families. In 1983, the boarding school became a day school and was opened to boys, as its capacity was expanded by the hiring of new teachers. In addition, the *mornes* saw the establishment of new, 'little schools', such as the one opened in Viaux in 1984 in a structure built by the villagers. This effort showed that a community could mobilize to improve the prospects of all its children. (Viaux is a hamlet that is a two-hour walk from the centre of Fonds-des-Nègres.)

New students

Over the course of their visits to the *mornes* for outdoor library sessions, the volunteers met many children who were not in school because they were too poor. They enrolled them on a priority basis for the following school year. The school's capacity was increased several times. One hundred additional children were admitted for the 1987 school year, and 60 more in 1993, including children who were already 8, 9 or 10 years old. Concern for the poorest was widely shared by the population as a whole. Families with slightly greater resources than others agreed to enrol only one of their children in this school since the others could go elsewhere, thereby making room in the Pemel school for children from poorer families.

These new students were, of course, at a disadvantage because of their living conditions. Some walked more than an hour to school, very often on empty stomachs. On harvest or market days, they sometimes missed school because they were needed to help the family. Other absences were explained by illness (that of the child or of a family member requiring assistance) or by a death in the family. But the teachers, who knew the parents, understood the problems, and the children were always readmitted to class on their return. Schoolmates offered help, too.

An ambitious educational project despite scant resources

In the beginning, the school had no real textbooks. Nor did it have a 'curriculum'. All of this would come with time. The teachers knew simply that their job was to prepare these children for life and to improve their skills for coping with their environment and their means of expression. Priority was given to teaching literacy in Creole first and later in French, as well as to basic arithmetic. Much attention was also given to activities requiring imagination (such as stories, drawing and games) and to everything that might contribute to their discovery of nature and the world around them, with an emphasis on what Haitian farmers and craftsmen do. Gardening projects were also organized. The goal was to teach the children pride in their own background and environment and to encourage a desire to be of use in the development of their country.

New teachers

In the beginning, the school did not have qualified staff because it could not pay the same salary as the officially recognized schools. Classes were taught by the sons and daughters of peasant farmers or small merchants. Among them, some had finished primary school and, occasionally, a few years of secondary school. At first they were able to teach what they themselves had learned. But very soon they began to feel inadequate because of their lack of training as teachers. Some would resign at year-end or even in mid-year. Not all resignations were motivated by this feeling of inadequacy. There were other reasons, such as illness or a move to a different location. All of these factors contributed to attrition, which made it difficult to put together a faculty that was sufficiently stable and stimulating. At the beginning of the 1988-1989 school year, for example, the Pemel school had 14 classes with four teachers who had been on staff for three to five years, six teachers for one year or less and four newly hired teachers. Assembling a group of competent, motivated and committed teachers capable of one day taking responsibility for what was intended to become a fully recognized school was a constant concern.

These new teachers also feared the judgements of their peers and comparisons or training that would bring out aspects of their incompetence. In the beginning, at least, it was hard for them to accept training sessions on teaching methods, pupil evaluation and preparing for meetings with the parents. This was especially true when these sessions took place out of school hours, since, because of their low wages, many teachers were forced to moonlight: for example, running a stall in the market in order to support their families.

Those who were able to stay with the school gradually developed a new perception of the children and of the importance of education. They became willing to put more energy into teaching and to help each other in their efforts to improve. They even took a certain pride in their social and professional commitment:

- "Teaching these children makes me feel useful. I am doing something concrete to change the future of the country."
- "This school is like a big family. The children feel at home."
- "I'm staying, and I'm devoting myself to poor children" (from a teacher who could earn twice as much at another school).

In June 1984, the visit of a school district inspector who was very favourably impressed by the work done at the Pemel school gave new impetus to improving the teachers' training, with the following results:

- thanks to various courses offered for their benefit (typing, advanced spelling, English, French, etc.) and to the opening of a library that allowed them to hold book-based learning sessions with the children, the teachers became better equipped to teach and more confident;
- thanks to the technical assistance provided from 1985 to 1987 by a French husband-and-wife teaching team, higher professional standards evolved that were maintained after the couple left;
- thanks to the added presence of a doctor who had joined the team of volunteers in 1988, the teachers were able to improve

their knowledge of health issues, and hygiene courses were introduced in the classroom;

- thanks to the collaboration of the Centre Labordes, the training centre for parochial school teachers in southern Haiti, the teachers participated in short courses and Centre Labordes instructors visited the school to provide teaching assistance. The Centre is a Haitian organization that endeavours to place every human resource available in Haiti for teacher training at the service of its poorest children.

At the same time, the team of volunteers was anxious to provide teaching assistance to the isolated teachers in the 'little schools' in the *mornes,* who, often single-handedly, provided a schooling to which the families had become very attached. Since 1984, two 'little schools' connected with the Pemel school, the Viaux and Pélissier schools, had been receiving particular attention and support from the volunteers. In 1988-1989, the Viaux 'little school' had one teacher and one teacher's aide for 113 students. The Pélissier school had one teacher for 67 students.

Parents become partners

While the participation of parents in their children's schooling increased yearly, the parents had made an effort to contribute from the very start, by providing vegetables for the school lunches or by donating a symbolic *gourde* (the national currency unit, approximating FF1.30 or 0.20 dollar) each month for school expenses. Parents also provided the necessary back-to-school supplies, and some did not hesitate to beg for that purpose. Those who were able to bought the textbooks that were indispensable to the school or rented them in the case of the higher grades. A sliding payment scale was developed for others.

Parents accompanied their children to school twice a year for the handing out of report cards. Each teacher tried to speak with the child's parents. Since 1983, quarterly meetings with the parents were held for every class. If a family was not represented at these meetings, the teachers and volunteers would call at the house. This was also the practice when a child was ill or absent for a long period of time. The innovative introduction of home visits helped to establish good relations between the school and the families. Parents who had been visited were less reluctant to meet with teachers at the school itself.

In fact, it took an extensive period of time and great perseverance to convince parents to express their opinions concerning the content of the curriculum, especially since most had never been to school themselves. Imagine what 'participating' means, for example, to a landless family that begs for a living and has seven children, none of whom have ever gone to school. One day the school offers to admit the three oldest girls and their younger brother the following school year. The father is astounded by this offer. He agrees, even in the case of his eldest daughter, who is a very valuable helper to her mother. Because of malnutrition, only this eldest daughter is actually able to finish the school year. Despite the period of mourning imposed by the death of one of her little brothers, her parents allow her to take her final exams, which she passes. For her father, this is a great discovery. His eldest daughter has succeeded and will be able to write for the family. This means that all of his children could potentially succeed. "Now he comes to the parents' meetings. There was a time when he spoke with his head down. Now he shows his face when he speaks. You can look him in the eye. He is a different man."

The first attempt to set up a parents' committee was made during the 1989-1990 school year. In each class, a parent was invited to work with the teacher to prepare the meeting with the parents. In fact, the first attempt failed because the teachers were unsure of themselves. It took three more years and the assistance of instructors from the Centre Labordes, who came to explain how this worked elsewhere, for the teachers not to feel threatened and for a real collaboration to be established between the parents' committee (with one representative per zone) and the teachers' committee.

This collaboration was particularly close in the case of the 'little schools' in the *mornes*. For example, it was the parents who, during the school holidays, built or restored the lattice-work structures used for classrooms and took up a collection to pay for the land. In Viaux, in 1991, the parents even built a simple one-room house for the teacher, who was unable to make the trip back down to central Fonds-des-Nègres on a daily basis.

Evaluation

In 12 years, the Pemel school expanded its capacity to 850 children in classes from the preparatory level to the fifth year of primary school, taking some students up to the level of the *certificat d'études* (completion of primary school). The number of teachers increased from 2 (in 1981) to 24 (in 1992), of whom 3 work in Pélissier and 2 in Viaux. Progress was registered for the overall student body, as was attested to by visiting instructors and inspectors and by the fact that some students went on to pursue their education in other schools.

Above all, the school was henceforth a part of the lives of all of the families in the sense that it had become accessible to all of the children. This was thanks to the efforts of many people:

- the team of volunteers visiting the most isolated and excluded families,
- the young people who ran the outdoor libraries in the *mornes*,
- the teachers who agreed to stay on and worked to achieve a dialogue with the parents.

The primary focus consisted in doing everything possible to give children who did not go to school at all a chance to attend to whatever extent was feasible, enabling all of the students to go as far in their studies as possible despite their families' difficult circumstances. Because it was never possible for those in charge of the school to be certain in advance that their circumstances would allow the children to remain in school, they treated each school year as if it might be a pupil's last. This entailed assigning the best teachers to the youngest pupils so that the children with the least chance of continuing their education would receive the best instruction.

To this day, the school remains poor in material resources; the teachers earn less than elsewhere; the children attend free and receive partial board. However, it is a pilot or experimental school in the sense that it is intended and structured to accept children from every family. Nicknamed 'The Family School', it has succeeded in training teachers who are able to accommodate the poorest families, both the children and their parents, and find them a place in an educational structure.

It is the pursuit of this goal year by year that contributed the most to creating a spirit of community in this rural locality and to inspiring a new desire among young people to help those who had the most trouble keeping up. In 1993, ATD Fourth World's team of volunteers was able to consider pulling out of the project. Cooperation between the school (the administrators and the teachers' committee) and the families (the parents' committee) had become well enough established for the venture to continue on its own. Furthermore, agreement had been reached on extending access to education to benefit all the children.

This experiment shows that a project to provide schooling can succeed with teachers who initially lack real professional training and parents whose poverty blinds them to any vision of change. This challenge was taken on thanks to the shared belief of a group of people in the possibility of imparting a new perspective of solidarity in one of the key areas for combating underdevelopment and extreme poverty: access to learning. The duration of the commitment inspired by this shared conviction was also decisive. It takes long years of unflagging effort to put out signals and provide proof that the poorest families can also play a role in development, given an opportunity and sustained outside support.

CASE STUDY SUMMARIES

Bangkok, Thailand

Case study (summary)

- A cultural process: Reaching families whose poverty is central to their very existence

Overall context

With an annual growth rate of around 10 per cent, Thailand is one of South-east Asia's group of newly industrialized countries. Its capital, Bangkok, has experienced tremendous growth in the past decade; 20 per cent of its population lives in shanty towns. This rapid development provides hope for the inhabitants of the entire region, but it has not had a generalized or lasting effect on the poorest segments of the population.

Specific context

The families targeted by the project were living in a shanty town in particularly acute poverty. Approximately 200 families lived in cramped shelters made of salvaged materials that had been built directly on the ground, despite the presence of stagnant water. Most of the dwellings had no water or electricity. A third of the population came from the north-east of the country and had arrived over the preceding five years. Half was from Bangkok itself and had been living in the shanty town for 10 to 15 years. The constant threat of eviction and their inability to pay the rent, which in some cases was due daily, forced families to move from one place to another in the shanty town.

In order to survive, many residents engaged in salvage-related activities. Some hired themselves out to perform dangerous work.

All of a family's energy and ingenuity went into day-to-day survival. Those living in the shanty town were held in contempt. The shanty town was, in fact, a shelter for people who were accepted nowhere else. It should also be noted that life expectancy there was appreciably lower than among the rest of the population.

Objectives

- Reaching the children, young people and families most harshly affected by poverty within a shanty town population where all were beset by poverty;
- Enabling them to acquire the means to open up to the outside world and express themselves;
- Setting up a cultural initiative—designed to foster the sharing of knowledge between these very poor people and people from all social milieus, as well as between the very poor and existing structures—that would be rooted in the struggle, on the part of the very poor and of the country itself, to fight poverty.

Methodology

Getting to know a country 'from the bottom up'

In 1979, after six months in Cambodian refugee camps with the French Red Cross, several ATD Fourth World volunteers offered their services to an organization called the Human Development Centre. This organization was working to meet the needs of shanty town dwellers in the areas of education, health and housing, with an emphasis on housing.

One of the volunteers, a nurse, worked with a doctor from the organization in Bangkok's biggest shanty town, Khlong Toey (population 60,000). This is a site of historic importance to the country. Indeed, many migrants attracted by the harbour and the modern capital have settled here. It has also been a centre for social work for over 30 years. Another volunteer, a sociologist by training, studied Thailand's situation and undertook research in publications and at the university in order to improve her understanding of the country's quest for peace and harmony.

This initial inquiry pointed up the necessity of joining the people in their efforts to combat the problems created by poverty and to improve their future. This could only be achieved by sharing their lives. For the team, a new phase was opening, that of immersion.

The immersion phase

Attempting to reach the poorest by sharing their lives does not necessarily entail settling down in a specific place. Although poor families try to organize their lives in such a way as to assert their right to exist, the poorest are without roots and often homeless. How, then, were they to be reached?

In 1984, the team began with a travelling street library that followed the movements of families known to its members. Through these street libraries, the children could express their hunger for learning and the extraordinary strength of their family ties. The street libraries were tangible public evidence of the team's determination to reach the poorest. A street library would also travel at the instigation of very poor families, who would urge the team to go to various places that they knew to be particularly neglected. In 1988, people living in the streets were able to alert the team to the presence of a small shanty town that had grown up near a bridge, where some 200 families lived.

The years 1988 and 1989 were marked by a closer proximity to the families in this particularly poor slum. The team witnessed suffering, health problems, begging, police raids, drugs, scholastic failure, a constant search for odd jobs in the attempt to survive, and parents who were unable to assume their responsibilities, which led to many children being taken into foster care. But the team also witnessed the efforts of these families in such a poverty-stricken environment. The team discovered social ties between the most disadvantaged and the segments of the population with more security. Many people were in fact anxious to re-establish harmony between the victims of poverty and the rest of society.

The Art and Poetry workshop

It was decided to set up an Art and Poetry workshop in the shanty town itself. This was a challenge in view of the people's everyday lives. It is important to bear their very real circumstances in mind in order to understand clearly the significance of participating in a workshop of this kind. It was more than a place to learn. Families who participated found a new way of communicating their thoughts and feelings. It gave them an opportunity to reveal themselves to others through their ideas and plans and most cherished values; in other words, through something other than the hardships generated by poverty.

By 1992, the time was ripe to move the workshop outside the shanty town in order to offer the families a greater range of opportunities to escape the confines of poverty. This move was made possible by the trust that had been built between the families and the team. A house was rented in a neighbourhood close by. This project was the result of collaboration between ATD Fourth World and the Ministry of Labour, with the support of the International Labour Office. The name of the house, 'Creativity and Encounter Centre', is an accurate reflection of the activities that take place on its premises. They include:

- discussion sessions bringing adults together to reflect upon their lives and experiences;
- workshops for children and young people during which artists and professionals pass along basic techniques and know-how;
- many meetings with various community members (neighbours, social workers and teachers, for example), reflecting the desire on both sides to work together to fight poverty.

The Centre was officially inaugurated on 2 May 1993 in a ceremony presided over by a Buddhist priest, with representatives of the city and international and non-governmental organizations in attendance. The participation of families from various shanty towns proved essential.

Lessons to be learned

Obstacles to participation

The following elements have been clearly identified as obstacles:

- the rootlessness of the families, who are constantly forced to move from one dwelling or shanty town to another;
- the precarious nature of their living conditions and employment prospects, and the resulting insecurity;
- the fact that they constitute a population that is often despised and automatically suspected of criminal activity;
- the fact that people living in extreme poverty are commonly thought to be incapable of appreciating beauty, and certainly unable to express themselves in cultural terms.

Observations made

a) the role of the poorest in facilitating an effort by indicating where those who are even poorer can be found;

b) the presence of non-poor people with a lasting commitment to the population living in the shanty town;

c) the role of Buddhist values (peace, harmony, tolerance and freedom), as well as that of the country's efforts to integrate all social groups into modern society, in lending meaning to individual gestures of assistance and solidarity;

d) the proof that, working with poor families, it is possible to re-establish dignified social ties between these families and the rest of society;

e) the certainty acquired *in vivo* that, to change the circumstances of the poorest, conditions must be created in which they can publicly demonstrate their belief in values recognized by the population as a whole. The Art and Poetry workshop was at the core of this project.

A dual approach: Sharing the lives of the poorest and rallying resources around them

a) The time spent with the people in their daily lives was proof of a desire for more than a superficial acquaintance and of a determination to establish relationships of trust and even friendship with the poorest. By suggesting activities that, in spite of the obstacles of daily life, allowed dialogue, self-expression and the creation of beautiful and useful things, the volunteers helped restore their human dignity to those who participated.

b) The process set in motion by the street libraries and followed up with the Art and Poetry workshop brought in people from outside the shanty towns. This encounter between the universe of poverty and the rest of society, as well as the dialogue that arose from it, signalled a common desire to live together again in peace, harmony and mutual understanding. As a result of this understanding, both sides came to see that the poorest could be full participants in society.

Cuzco, Peru

Case study (summary)

- A university initiative to carry out research/action in collaboration with a very poor rural community

Context

This project is concerned with small rural communities in isolated areas of the Pisaq district in the province of Calca. Those who live in these steep, mountainous regions work under particularly difficult conditions. Harvests depend on the weather. Hunger is a constant threat, and the people have to resort to various means of survival, including diversifying their agricultural resources, moving to urban centres or forested areas to work and developing small businesses, especially handicrafts.

In 1976, a professor of anthropology from the University of Cuzco began visiting these rural communities, at times accompanied by colleagues. He encouraged his students to spend time there, and he himself lived in the area for long periods of time, befriending the farm workers and learning from them about their history, their way of life and their efforts.

In 1980, he launched a research/action project that he called *Transforming the Campesino Economy in the Vilcanota Region: Calca, Quispicanchis and Canchis.* He was able to undertake this project because of his awareness of the very difficult living and working conditions of the farmer labourers, the ties he had formed with them, and also because of his commitment, which had grown steadily over the years. His research was backed by the United Nations and had the financial support of the universities of Tilburg, Amsterdam and Leiden, in the Netherlands.

Objectives

The goal of this research/action project was to identify the requirements for transforming the campesino economy. Its purpose was to develop a process whereby everyone, campesinos and academics alike, would become 'researchers'. Its objectives were:

- to foster the active participation—and transformation—of all of the parties involved in developing a common understanding and analysis of the socio-economic situation;
- to define a method of applied research/action that could be used in designing other development projects.

Methodology

a) The objectives were based on the conviction that, for too long, many studies had treated the farm labourers as objects and that the time had come to treat them as partners. This meant acquiring an in-depth knowledge of their daily lives and culture, which in turn entailed identifying those objectives that could lead to developing a research/action methodology. For the professor, his colleagues and the students involved in the study, all of this meant living in these communities on a regular basis and participating in their activities. They would also gather and systematize socio-economic data.

b) After two years (1980-1982), the university cut off funding on the pretext that the experiment had gone on long enough. Clarifying the substance of the project became imperative. Was this a case of research conducted by persons who, regardless of the integrity of their motives, remained foreign to the community? Or was it a matter of continuing a process already set in motion that appeared to be leading to changes in the campesinos' self-image, their self-confidence and the way they used their abilities? What should be done about an innovative process rooted in the knowledge and realities of the farm workers?

c) For the professor, the answer was clear. He chose to remain faithful to his commitment to the campesinos and to do everything possible not to lose their trust or betray their hopes. Of course, the loss of funding seriously handicapped the project. He nevertheless invested his own money in order to continue to be near the campesinos, to visit them, to live with them and to work with them on various projects, even if his visits were at times less frequent. It is interesting to note that some of the young campesinos involved in the research went on to become decision makers in their communities.

d) In 1987, the professor participated in an ATD Fourth World international congress entitled "The Family, Extreme Poverty and Development". This meeting, he writes, represented a turning point in his efforts to reach *all* of the members of these campesino communities. In the course of later research/action projects, he came to realize that, in communities in which everyone is poor, some are not only poorer than others but, as a result of the higher degree of poverty, are also gradually pushed to the fringes and do not participate in decisions or discussions concerning the community's future.

Lessons to be learned

Identifying the poorest

In evaluating this research it became clear how families living in extreme poverty in a rural community were identified. Significant differences between comfortably well-to-do, moderately poor and poor campesinos were found in what had previously appeared to be a socially homogeneous group. Three observations were made:

- identification was made after a period of 11 years spent with the communities in question;
- it was after participation in the 1987 international conference that focused on the question of extreme poverty;
- lastly, certain signs were present that indicated extreme poverty:
  - a mother on her own because the father has died or is forced into temporary migration as a day labourer;

- a family deprived of land or savings;
- a family not participating in community meetings.

The evaluation prompted the following comments:

a) If we do not ask ourselves the specific question: "Who are the poorest?", are we not refusing to recognize their existence or think about their particular predicament, whether in terms of their family life, the resources available to them or their participation in society? In the absence of such a question, the differentiated character of poverty is lost: If we limit our view of poverty as pertaining to a single homogenous group, we cannot identify the poorest.

b) Working meetings that focus on the topic of the poorest and bring together field workers and researchers involved in the fight against poverty are few and far between. Until recently, such meetings received scant encouragement on the part of international organizations.

Time-frame of outside funding

We have already stressed the adverse consequences of funding being cut off while field research is still going on because the donor considers that the project has gone on long enough (in this case, two years).

It should be added that field workers and researchers working with very poor groups are often forced to adapt to requirements, conditions and criteria imposed by the private or public organizations that fund them. All too often, these organizations underestimate the quality and quantity of human investment needed to acquire an in-depth knowledge of a culture or of the characteristics of the very poor and their traditions with respect to freedom and solidarity. Without a real understanding of the social and cultural realities of the very poor, how can a programme hope to bring about a lasting change in the conditions impeding their development? Changes measurable in the short term are required in order to justify the assistance granted. But this requirement can cancel out the real idea behind development, which involves going beyond simply satisfying a few basic needs identified on the basis of quantitative criteria.

Role and responsibilities of those working to establish a partnership with the poorest

This project raises a number of questions both for universities and for organizers of community programmes:

a) Should a university not institute a permanent research programme to study the socio-economic problems of the poorest segments of the population? Should not researchers make the hopes and questions of the poorest their own and acknowledge the ability of the very poor to contribute to the solution?

b) Should not non-governmental organizations avoid imposing a form of development or supplying their own, independently devised solutions? Failing this, would they not be running the risk of creating a bureaucracy that relies solely on the better-off members of the community for the success of their projects and invests only in partial aspects of progress?

In fact, researchers and field workers must work together to improve the use of human and material resources, preferably through small projects, not only to satisfy priority needs and make contact with the most socially excluded groups, but also to provide a means of active participation for every member of the community.

Jinja, Uganda

Case study (summary)

- A rural initiative: Monitoring and activism in the service of those who are in greatest need

Overall context

Walukuba Estates, with a population of approximately 30,000, is the largest housing complex in Uganda. It is situated on Lake Victoria, about 6 km from Jinja, the country's second largest city. Development of Walukuba began in 1948 in order to provide housing for factory workers in the Jinja area, to which people were flocking to find work in the hope of improving their living conditions. The houses were soon divided up so that rooms could be sublet. In many of them today, whole families live in a single room.

Most of the factories have since closed. Deprived of this source of income, the people survive by doing 'odd jobs'. A recent drought, higher taxes and rising inflation have combined to aggravate the situation. In addition to the diseases prevalent in this part of Africa, AIDS poses a major public health problem.

On the positive side, the Christian and Muslim communities coexist peacefully, and the end of ethnic strife has brought a measure of security.

Specific context

For the inhabitants of Walukuba, finding a job that pays enough to support a family is difficult, and many men are obliged to leave the community. Some mothers are also forced to leave their children, working outside the home in order to bring in a little money. Children themselves work to help out their families.

The poorest families live in insanitary temporary housing. The living conditions, poor sanitation and malnutrition all have a very negative impact on the health of the people. The very poor have little access to medical services. School fees are too high for them, and they have to choose between feeding their children and sending them to school.

In the face of such circumstances, some, among them children, are driven to resort to ways of getting money that they cannot admit to one another. Family unity is threatened. Some people end up on the streets.

Objectives

To experience within the community a solidarity that includes all of its members, however poor. To that end, the following goals were devised:

- to monitor and identify the needs of the most disadvantaged inhabitants on a constant basis;
- to foster new commitments and responsibilities for the purpose of meeting those needs;
- to strengthen social ties within the community as well as with the surrounding society for the purpose of promoting development for and by all.

Methodology

The Walukuba Mission has a small health dispensary, several storage sheds, a large room suitable for classes, a community hall and a small guest house. It also has three huts on the outskirts of the Mission that house elderly people. The Mission was founded in 1970 by a Catholic priest from Uganda. He is assisted by a man who grew up in Walukuba. The other members of the Mission team are a registered nurse, who runs the dispensary, and a man whose principal responsibility is to be a community liaison. All the team members live in Walukuba.

The Mission's principal resources

The team can count on very few material resources. The principal resources are human: the members of the permanent team and those people from the community who help implement the various projects initiated by the Mission.

This lack of resources makes the work difficult. In addition to running the Mission dispensary, the nurse must hold down a job at the hospital in order to feed her family. However, she often stays on at the dispensary beyond her scheduled hours in order to keep it open and provide treatment for those who need it. Efforts of this kind are not always recognized. For example, a woman employed by the diocese to evaluate the medical programmes suggested closing the dispensary. She thought that the patient load of approximately 20-30 people a day could be handled by the medical facility in Jinja. This opinion failed to take into account the obstacles that prevent the very poor from obtaining medical services. The fact is that closing the dispensary would deprive the very poor of any medical care at all.

The elementary school classes are another example of how the community can get together to find solutions to its most pressing needs. In this way, classes held by two young men help the most disadvantaged families, who cannot afford to send their children to other schools.

Joining with the poorest in projects that will help the whole community

There is no secondary school to serve the Walukuba Estates—the nearest is in Jinja, and too expensive for many residents. The Mission has decided to build one with the help of the residents, although it has not been able to do so yet. The challenge for the secondary school project is to make sure that the poorest—the families who do not have the means to pay school fees and whose children spend their time scavenging in the dustbins on the streets of Jinja—have their place in the project.

Giving the whole community a voice

The team has also been very active in promoting the formation of a community association that would represent Walukuba Estates in its dealings with city officials. The goal was twofold: to create an awareness of the situation of the neighbourhood's residents and to establish the conditions for partnership between the residents and the people with whom they deal outside the community.

Involving the poorest in the country's priorities

The Mission launched a number of projects corresponding to the country's defined priorities, making sure at the same time that the poorest were granted a true part in those initiatives. One way to do this was by means of an agricultural project in keeping with the national policy of reviving the people's interest in farming. Also significant was the fact that all the members of the community gathered to discuss the country's new Constitution.

International solidarity

In the view of the team running the initiative, it was important for those contributing to the projects to understand that they were part of a broad movement of solidarity with the poorest. When requested to participate in the 'Reaching the poorest' study, the priest who founded the Mission asked: "Why would UNICEF want to know about such a small project as ours?" But he added: "If these two levels of development and exchange can discover each other in a relationship of mutual trust, the main beneficiaries will be the poorest."

Lessons to be learned

The priest in charge of the Mission has been in this community for 24 years. This long-term commitment has allowed him to acquire knowledge and experience, and provides a solid foundation on which other community members can build. He embodies an ideal, as well as the memory of a struggle to bring everyone into the social life of the community. This is not an easy battle to wage. In a community where each person's circumstances are very insecure, how can anyone allow himself the luxury of solidarity with the poorest?

The priest's role was to try to get the community to practise solidarity with the most disadvantaged in spite of the tremendous difficulties experienced by the whole community. Inspired by the momentum he was able to summon up, he considered instituting and running universally accessible community services. However, such an action is unlikely to lead to lasting results if local efforts are not matched by outside support.

The collaboration of international organizations in local efforts led by organizers with deep roots in their communities would unquestionably mean that indeed the poorest would be reached and appropriate responses made to their most urgent needs; it would also serve to consolidate their social integration while strengthening overall community unity.

Rouyn-Noranda and Montreal, Canada

Case study (summary)

- A civic action: Citizens show their solidarity in the struggle against poverty

Overall context

In a climate of economic recession, the impoverishment of the country's middle and working classes is increasingly overshadowing the fate of its poorest citizens. Training programmes, for example, are less and less accessible to those with only a few years of primary education. The growth of poverty has created new categories of problems. The country is dealing with them by multiplying the number of specialists involved. Despite increased rhetoric about poverty and impoverishment, the poor themselves have very little opportunity to speak out. The economically stressed middle classes criticize the welfare recipients. This reinforces prejudices and prevents the emergence of a collective awareness of the urgency of uniting to combat poverty.

During the Great Depression, many families fleeing poverty and hunger moved from Montreal to Rouyn-Noranda, the economic capital of the Abitibi-Temiscamingue region (800 km northwest of Montreal). This region owes its development to mining but has always had a history of poverty. Unemployment affects many families. Family life is often disrupted. A feeling of uselessness prevails among the jobless, who are dependent on government welfare benefits to feed their families.

Objectives

- To create a civic action bringing citizens from every social background to the side of the poorest in order to express and foster a joint rejection of poverty.
- To identify the following elements:
  a) those factors that hinder, as well as those that promote, the participation of very poor families in private or public programmes geared towards them;
  b) the kind of support that is necessary for the poorest to take advantage of these programmes;
  c) the type of training that should be given to the various programme managers and social workers.

Methodology

Crossroads

In 1989, a local association called Rouyn-Noranda Crossroads was founded in the Abitibi region to bring together people from different social backgrounds. The aim of this association was to provide a supportive environment and a springboard to empower people still trapped in poverty to claim their role as citizens recognized by their community. The association presents itself as a group that does not depend on welfare but tries instead to promote solidarity. The people who join Crossroads help each other to learn or relearn solidarity with poor people and others who are convinced, as they are, that poverty can be defeated.

A number of factors have been decisive in this effort:

a) *Providing mutual support in grappling with poverty.* The Crossroads quickly became central to those involved in it. Above and beyond providing a welcoming environment, it affords members the opportunity to feel useful to others by contributing ideas and energy.

b) *Training, taking initiatives and carrying out responsibilities.* In spite of their poverty, Crossroads members have never stopped fighting to defend their dignity and to improve their children's prospects. Crossroads has become a place for regaining one's strength and a forum for organizing mutual support initiatives. Members have gradually found the strength to reach out to those who are poorer than they and to help break their isolation. Each member has contributed to moving the group forward. Together, they have sought to form alliances with people in welfare offices, local organizations and their children's schools. In this way they are helping to find more equitable solutions to the problems they face.

c) *Dialogue and action with other partners.* The group has demonstrated its desire to engage in dialogue and reflection with others through a variety of initiatives. For example, Crossroads participated in an assessment of food distribution activities. Members took the time to meet with the recipients and were able to gain their trust. They discovered that people found the food distribution humiliating but did not dare say so or make suggestions for improving the system for fear that it would be discontinued. No survey conducted by the distribution organizers had ever mentioned this.

d) *Trying another approach to fighting poverty.* Crossroads members first learned how to become spokespersons for others, and in particular the very poor. Next, they helped train social workers. This has not been easy and has taken much time. In general, they have sought to invent new ways of increasing awareness of the conditions imposed on the very poor.

e) *Forming alliances to reject poverty.* This has been one of the fundamental points. People from more well-to-do segments of the population have agreed to participate in the group's activities and to contribute their know-how. In the beginning, some came to help. They soon realized that they had been invited to participate in an exchange and that it had an impact on their own lives. Joining with the poor in rejecting poverty led them to make a significant gesture on 17 October 1993, when they dedicated a commemmorative stone to the victims of poverty. It was a replica of the one dedicated on 17 October 1987 by Father Joseph Wresinski at the Trocadéro in Paris.

'Reaching the Poorest'

The group that goes by this name was founded in Montreal in 1992. It consists of social workers, community representatives, clergy and heads of programmes serving the disadvantaged. The goal of its members is to serve as a think tank to determine whether their respective activities provide support for the poorest and to what extent these activities truly reach the poorest.

This group has identified a number of points:

a) *The burden of urgency*: Many people involved with very poor families come up against serious problems requiring urgent measures (for example, housing, food or medical care). In such circumstances, it is difficult for them to assess what these families' plans might be or what efforts they are already making.

b) *Conditions for moving from assistance to partnership*: Bearing in mind the urgency factor and the difficulty of making the public aware that the poorest deal actively each day with the problems that they encounter, the group's members have identified a number of conditions for enabling them to become partners:

1. building trust between the very poor and others, which requires them to know one another;
2. developing projects that break down prejudices and bring people together;
3. taking a comprehensive approach, in contrast with the current tendency, which is to bring in more and more people and offer increasingly fragmented solutions;
4. making evaluation a joint process.

Lessons to be learned

A certain number of conditions must be fulfilled in order to enable the very poor and those working with them to give public expression to their suggestions as to what action should be taken; indeed, without the input of a perspective that is unique to the very poor, no one can presume to eradicate extreme poverty. These conditions can be divided into three categories:

1) *Conditions for fostering the participation of the very poor*

- They must find a way to provide each other with mutual support and to secure the support of others;
- They must be able to develop and strengthen their personal identities;
- They must arrive at a common understanding of how to go about demonstrating the unfairness of certain situations and developing solutions;
- They must be led to take initiatives and exercise responsibilities.

2) *Conditions for ensuring a responsible commitment to the very poor*

- Being able to give one another mutual support;
- Having a suitable place to meet and the means to reflect together on the best ways to promote partnership with the poorest populations in the light of shared experience and current circumstances.

3) *Conditions for building a partnership between the poorest and the rest of society*

- Willingness to take the time to meet the very poor and to get to know one another;
- Willingness to avoid presenting fully elaborated projects, but to develop them together as a group;
- Reliance on the strengths of very poor families;
- Identification of common objectives and individual responsibilities (for poor families, volunteers and government);

- Emphasis on making provision for training. Poor people wish for training in order to be able to take on responsibilities. As for the training of those working with the poorest, it should go beyond theoretical aspects to include the vast pool of experiences accumulated by the poorest;
- Care in setting up opportunities and forums for dialogue between the different partners;
- A vision of the very poor as partners across the board, which involves consulting with them and listening to them on issues broader than the struggle against poverty, on matters that are of importance to the future of the world, such as the environment, peace, cultural development, the family and democracy.

CONCLUSION

To conclude this study, it should be remembered that poverty is in and of itself the greatest obstacle to reaching the poorest. Poverty undermines family security and destroys social ties within the community. It prevents participation in development. It isolates and excludes its victims. Nevertheless, this study shows that programmes can be developed that not only reach the poorest but also collaborate with them as real partners.

Reaching the poorest does not mean grouping them so as to single them out within a community or neighbourhood. On the contrary, the approach should be made within the framework of overall development conceived of by the community as a whole, so as to ensure that each member takes an active part in the development process, being at once a beneficiary and a participant. We have seen that if a programme does not take the poorest members of the community into consideration from the outset, it will be very difficult to include them at a later stage, and the gap between the poorest and the rest of the community is likely to grow. For this reason, the needs of the community and those of its poorest members should be considered together and integrated into a single, consensus-based programme. In this context, there is a close link between respect for the rights of the individual (and thus the poorest) and respect for the rights of the community as a whole.

There are three immediate lessons to be derived from the projects dealt with in this study:

1) In order to reach the poorest and enable them to become real partners, it is necessary to know them in depth. Yet their circumstances cause them to lead isolated, at times hidden, lives.

One must therefore take the time to seek them out. Furthermore, experience shows that the poorest do not express their innermost thoughts immediately. First of all, they lack the means to do so, and, second, a relationship of trust must be established before they can engage in real dialogue with others. Where this trust exists, we see that they do not speak about their poverty in terms of needs and problems but rather in terms of events, suffering and resistance. It is this history that shapes their thoughts and fuels their expectations, hopes and efforts.

2) The poorest survive first and foremost by their own efforts, as evidenced by the countless actions taken by fathers, mothers, young people and children living in extreme poverty. These actions are performed for their own benefit, but also for that of their families and neighbours. To remain capable of providing shelter for a mother forced out into the streets with her children when one is oneself living in cramped, insecure quarters is an example of the kind of gesture that allows the poorest to survive.

3) A community that is generally poor spends little time talking about its poorest members. Including the poorest poses difficulties, particularly when prospects arise for improvement, as in the case of a development project. Under such circumstances, the community will tend to exclude the poorest because, owing to their extreme poverty, they are unable to take part in the project and could thereby compromise it. Yet the project is aimed at the overall community, which is not comfortable with this dismissal of the poorest. This study shows that the community suffers from having to inflict such a rejection and seeks ways of remedying the situation. Whatever the setting, it is possible to find support for carrying out a community programme that excludes no one.

Acquiring a genuine knowledge of what extreme poverty is like and building solidarity with all the members of a community requires time and entails creating the conditions for real closeness. This approach might be more typical of that deployed by non-governmental organizations, in that it allows them to fulfil their roles as witnesses and innovators. It is in the NGOs that we find people who have the training and willingness needed to share in the difficulties and rejections that mark a project attempting to make the poorest full partners.

This study has led the different partners—UNICEF, International Movement ATD Fourth World, the local organizers of the seven projects and the communities involved—to reflect more deeply on the form that a commitment to the poorest should take. The strategies of these partners truly complement one another. They have also noted that there are still too few opportunities for international bodies and small, locally active organizations to get to know each other or share their experiences. In this connection, we have seen in the first part of this book that one of the objectives of the Permanent Forum on Extreme Poverty in the World is to make the voices of small organizations heard and their experiences known. This Permanent Forum is currently in a position to identify those people and small organizations throughout the world that are the keystones of development rooted in the local community and attentive to the inclusion of the very poor. As a follow-up to this study, thought should be given to how to identify and support such initiatives.

The ongoing exchanges among the partners, the basis of this study, have made all of them aware that they are facing a challenge which they must meet together: that of reaching the poorest in every aspect of their lives. NGOs can provide the field knowledge that is theirs through their closeness to the most disadvantaged. They have also often worked in partnership with the poorest, but at the community level. A United Nations-related agency such as UNICEF can provide an overall vision and its expertise as a key player in the social sector. It is close to national and international decision makers and is often in a position to exercise influence.

Together, these partners could launch one or more experimental programmes that would take the findings of this study as a point of departure and attempt to refine them, the goal being to reach the poorest on a wider scale. Such a project could help to lay the foundations of a policy for combating extreme poverty in partnership with the poorest on a scale that NGOs are not always able to attain by themselves. As the study demonstrates, extreme poverty is universal and, beyond the characteristics specific to each context, exhibits characteristics common to all contexts. This universality motivates us to fight poverty not only through local policies but also through general policies involving the entire international community.

It is in this sense that the UNICEF Executive Board's decision entitled 'Reaching the poorest' sets a task for the entire international community. Extreme poverty was the focus of the attention of all the governments represented at the 1995 World Summit for Social Development in Copenhagen. In proclaiming 1996 the International Year for the Eradication of Poverty, the United Nations called for a platform bringing together all of the partners in economic, social and cultural development, as well as human rights, to increase what is known about the poorest and identify further ways of ensuring their full participation in world development. However, shouldn't attempts to reach the poorest give an echo to the philosophy of Father Joseph Wresinski? It was he who tirelessly reminded us, long before we began wondering how to reach the poorest, that the poorest were constantly wondering how to reach the society in which they lived.